MN

WITHDRAWN

AN AMERICAN
IN WASHINGTON

AN AMERICAN
IN
WASHINGTON

Russell Baker

ALFRED A. KNOPF · NEW YORK

1961

L. C. catalog card number: 61–13951

THIS IS A BORZOI BOOK,
PUBLISHED BY ALFRED A. KNOPF, INC.

FIRST EDITION

T O

Mimi

CONTENTS

1.   MORE DANGEROUS THAN MOSCOW   3

2.   THE NATIVES: *Their Work and Curious*
     Temperament   10

     The Importance of Despair

3.   THE SOCIETY: *How to Put on the Dog*
     without Pedigree   27

     The Urgency of Lunch
     Why the Cocktail Party
     Common Hostessing
     The Ritual Dinner
     Uncommon Hostessing
     Addenda

4. THE WHITE HOUSE   57

    How to Be a Great President
    The Survival Problem
    The Great Hagerty
    The Satisfying Misery

5. THE PRESIDENT'S 2,500,000 RIGHT ARMS   90

    The Bureaucrat's Duties
    Washingtonese: The Art of Obfuscating
    The President's Peril

6. DIPLOMATIC CIRCLES   116

    Getting Along with Congress
    Getting Along with Foreigners
    Getting Along with Americans
    Reacting
    Apologia

7. THE HILL   140

    Baroque-ialism
    The Persecuting Minority
    How to Be a Successful Senator
    The Not So Lower House
    Valedictory

8. IN TOGA AND GUMSHOE   172

    How to Be Investigated
    The Question

9. THE TATTLERS   192

    The White House News Conference
    Hindsighting and Crystal-Balling
    Esoterica

10. HAIL AND FAREWELL   226

AN AMERICAN
IN WASHINGTON

1

More Dangerous
than Moscow

Washington lies slightly south of Madrid and west of Maracaibo on a swamp littered with marble imitations of ancient Roman and Greek architecture.

Its tallest structure is an obelisk with which the United States honors its first President, who was not an Egyptian but an eighteenth-century colonial aristocrat and heir to a fortune built on slave labor.

The city was planned by a Frenchman. The majority of its inhabitants are of African descent. In one respect, all are in a class with conquered enemy aliens in occu-

3

pied territory: residence in Washington deprives them of the right of self-government.

Washingtonians come in all colors and nationalities, but no matter how disparate their origins, sooner or later all find a common bond in two things. In the summer it is the desperate contest between man and crab grass, a weed that flourishes with maddening virulence in the subtropical damp. The rest of the year it is politics, an occult art practiced by the city's famous, and incessantly discussed, though rarely understood, by everyone else.

Washington's chief industry is tourism, a degrading business that consists in being looked at, photographed, and rummaged by vaguely hostile aliens wearing ridiculous shirts and smoked glasses.

One of the city's most popular tourist attractions is the Federal Bureau of Investigation, one of several federal police headquarters, where the visitor may examine a large fingerprint file, inspect death masks of sundry hoodlums, and enjoy an exhibition of submachine-gun firing.

The city is also famous for Japanese cherry trees, which frame the view of a Roman pantheon memorializing Thomas Jefferson, a dangerous revolutionary who founded the Democratic party.

Physically, the city Washington most resembles is New Delhi. Both are artificial cities with broad shaded boulevards converging on traffic circles; both are characterized by massive stone piles in which the musty, sealing-wax business of government is conducted.

There is no conspicuous Mogul architecture in Washington, but there is a splendidly delicate Arabian mosque set at the top of an elm-covered hill. The Capitol dome, a local landmark, is a cast-iron imitation of Wren's on St. Paul's Cathedral in London. The White House, another landmark, is a copy of an eighteenth-century Irish mansion—Leinster House in Dublin. The Pentagon is an unabashed steal from Euclid, the Greek.

The memorial to Abraham Lincoln, a backwoodsman stigmatized by his contemporaries as a doltish rustic, is a Greek temple.

The Supreme Court is classic Greek with affidavit pomposity; the drabber federal office buildings, electronic-Roman; the private office buildings, cut-rate Le Corbusier.

Washington is bounded on the south by the Potomac River, which not only serves as the city's chief sewer and water-supply source but also provides a natural frontier with hot-tempered, underdeveloped Dixie. On the east, west, and north, artificial boundary lines mark its frontier with the United States.

Relations with both powers are usually strained, but like Switzerland, Washington is assured of safety from overpowering, testy neighbors by the mutual understanding that her neutral ground is more valuable as a

5

diplomatic, financial, and espionage center than as real estate.

Neither side has much use for Washington. North and South, it is generally despised as an unworthy place where men of mean talents but cunning proclivities conspire to inconvenience decent people beyond its frontiers.

According to custom, after the Americans have chosen a President he is required to come to Washington to work. Men campaigning for the presidency often find it helpful to exploit primitive American suspicions about the city and so travel through the country promising to work the American's vengeance on Washington.

In 1952 an astonishingly successful campaign was built on the slogan "Let's clean up the mess in Washington."

"Washington," Senator James O. Eastland declared in 1960, "is a literal cesspool of crime and violence."

"Yes," Senator Barry Goldwater said in 1959, "I fear Washington more than I do Moscow."

Few American politicians consider a campaign speech complete without a denunciation of "bureaucrats," a universally understood synonym for faceless Washington conspirators who are presumed responsible for whatever ails the electorate at any given time.

Considering the constant tension in relations with its powerful neighbors, it is not surprising that Washington minds its step. In deference to the official puritanism of the Yankees, it discourages all but the most desultory forms of local sin. Thus, it is unlawful to take liquor in a public place while standing erect, or in any position on Sunday. Night life is distinctly dispiriting for the casual visitor; anyone who has visited Bayeux after the tapestry has been locked up for the night may easily imagine the plight of the stranger roaming downtown Washington in search of diversion. Let him absently cross some deserted intersection when the traffic light is red, and he invites arrest for jaywalking.

Travelers may enter Washington without visa, passport, or customs inspection. (Maryland residents, however, are liable to criminal punishment if caught taking out more than one quart of Washington whiskey.) The easy passage into the city is a principal cause of the humiliation so many Americans suffer when they get to Washington, for it tempts them to assume that they are merely passing from one patch of friendly motherland to another. Such people are dangerously lulled, and Washington is no place for the lulled. Some of its most famous men have had knives placed so professionally in their backs that they have learned about it only by reading the next morning's newspapers.

These pages represent an effort to supply a little of the practical information essential for survival in Washington. There is no attempt to present the definitive work, or even to explore deeply the basic subject matter that should be understood before entering the city. For example, there is no discussion of how to disconcert overconfident lawyers from the bench of the Supreme Court. While important to potential Supreme Court justices, such information is too specialized for a general survey of this kind.

Each reader may feel the need of additional study to prepare himself for the specific milieu he plans to enter. Thus, the man coming to Washington to be investigated will find advice on how to upstage a congressional committee, which may inspire him to make his own investigation into the techniques of successful perjury.

What other kind of information should go into a basic survey? It will vary with the individual. The newly elected senator may want to familiarize himself with the art of the laying on of hands, or as the master political masseur, Lyndon Johnson, calls it, "pressing the flesh." The young person planning a civil service career may require instruction in exhausting the citizen caller. The budding Washington correspondent should know that the White House may be the graveyard of his career if he lacks the vocal stamina of a hog caller.

Everyone planning to live awhile in Washington should be aware of the supreme importance of lunch in the city's social fabric, as well as the techniques of name dropping so essential to eminence in whichever circle he may yearn to conquer. He should grasp the importance of Obfuscation, an art he must master if he is to be considered wise when he knows nothing. He should

8

know of the inestimable value of the "inside story," that precious morsel of unprinted gossip which is the *sine qua non* of conversational brilliance in grand salons and over the water cooler.

Even people determined never to set foot in Washington will find a study of Crystal-Balling and Hindsighting helpful to their understanding of the political news and useful for building a reputation for sagacity in their own communities.

In fact, the person willing to examine the natives dispassionately, to glance at their curious institutions and mores and the odd things they do, may conclude in the end that while Washington and Washingtonians are even sillier than he had thought, they are not half so sinister.

This, then, is a book dedicated to easing tensions between the United States of America and the District of Columbia.

2

The Natives:

Their Work and Curious Temperament

WHAT ARE they like, these Washingtonians? Very much as you and I would be if we found ourselves in the curious jobs that Washingtonians perform. Which is to say, cocksure and uncertain, devious and naïve, ebullient and melancholy, pompous and frivolous, bored, hard-working, shiftless, wide-eyed and tired of it all, full of dreams and schemes, and, without quite realizing it, a little absurd, for they are mostly common men distinguished largely by possession of uncommon jobs.

Let us try to catch the city in action and, through a

montage of events, to capture the essence of the Washingtonian at his daily routine. Here, with all incidents based on fact or sound probability, is the chronology of a fairly representative Washington day out of the recent past:

BETWEEN 6 AND 7 A.M.

Alarm clocks ring beside four senators running for the presidency. In the moment between rising and shaving, each yields to the dawn's awful intimation of mortality and asks himself: "Is it really worth it?"

At the White House the President of the United States rises, accidentally kicking to the floor the cowboy story with which he had read himself to sleep last night. Yawning at the dark silhouette of the Washington Monument visible from his bedroom window, he remembers that he must attend a "prayer breakfast" at the Mayflower Hotel with a prominent evangelist and twenty-three congressmen and then lunch with an asthmatic tyrant from the Middle East. Retrieving the cowboy story, he fleetingly recalls his boyhood dream of horseback living under prairie stars and asks himself: "What am I doing here?"

In a network television studio a television correspondent famous in eighty million living rooms edits the questions he will ask an equally famous labor leader who has been accusing the President of callousness to human suffering. The correspondent, who must do his stuff for breakfasting America, is in a suppressed rage, having just been advised by his New York office that the time allotted the interview has been cut from five to three minutes. The network producer believes that five minutes of the labor leader will kill the audience and has decided to lighten the show with a two-minute act by that new comic from the Coast who does funny monologues with a telephone.

The twenty-three congressmen who are to breakfast with the President rise. Five have hang-overs. Three require their wives to read aloud from the *Congressional Record* speeches that they delivered yesterday in the House of Representatives. These treat, respectively, of pornography in the mails, the depletion of oyster beds in the Chesapeake Bay, and Communist influences on African nationalism.

The Secretary of Defense ignores his alarm clock. This afternoon he must start on a flight to Asia to mollify the South Koreans and the Chinese Nationalists. This, he tells himself, entitles him to an unbudgeted thirty minutes of sleep.

The second assistant to the deputy to the Assistant Secretary of State for Inter-American Affairs scolds his wife. Later today he is to receive a medal for completing forty years of faultless service to the government. The ceremony will be conducted in the office of the deputy to the Assistant Secretary, and the second assistant must wear his frayed sports coat and slacks. His wife forgot to collect his suit last night from the cleaner's.

Two hundred thousand government workers eat breakfast. Most of them laugh discreetly at Herblock's cartoon in *The Washington Post*, which depicts the President in chaps and spurs astride Old Paint and galloping for the hills to escape the responsibility of the White House.

The Secretary of State gloats to his wife about his success in having foisted off the Asian tour upon the Secretary of Defense and decides to scare the French with an ambiguous statement at his news conference this afternoon. It never really works with the French, but then it never really hurts either.

At the Mayflower Hotel the President bows his head while the evangelist prays over the sausages. The President is thinking that perhaps he has been too tough lately toward the French and that he will say something pleasant about them at his news conference tomorrow.

At households throughout the city 40,000 men pause, before setting off to work, to inspect roses, azaleas, rhododendrons, forsythias, and brown spots in the lawn.

Two hoodlums subpoenaed to appear before a House investigating committee at 10 A.M. are rehearsed

13

by lawyers over coffee in the proper form for refusing to testify under the Fifth Amendment.

In a Pentagon cafeteria two officers exchange greetings in the coffee line. "Heard about the security-conscious secretary who left her Pentagon job to take a job with a bishop?" asks one. "She filed all his correspondence under two headings—Sacred and Top Sacred."

BETWEEN 8 AND 9 A.M.

In thousands of government offices millions of pieces of paper are put manually into transit between desk baskets.

At the White House the news teletype in the Press Secretary's office taps out a report that the head of a small African state has died on the Scandinavian leg of his world peace tour. The Press Secretary composes a message of condolence and orders it mimeographed for later issuance under the President's name.

The Senate Majority Leader tells his secretary to set up appointments with two aging senators about to retire. He will need their votes to arrange a tie vote on an important labor bill. The Vice-President, who hopes to become President, will have to vote to break the tie, thus infuriating either organized labor or organized business and, in either case, making the Majority Leader a very happy man.

The Vice-President, in his office just across the hall,

is being photographed accepting a citation from the Society for a Wetter West. The Vice-President, the citation declares, "has ever been a fighter in the cause of a more fully irrigated West."

BETWEEN 9 AND 10 A.M.

Approximately 100,000 government workers begin approximately 20,000 staff conferences that will last until lunch.

Two congressmen returning from the prayer breakfast are asked how the President looked. "Bad," says one. "Never better," says another.

"Let's have some coffee," suggest 125,000 people, more or less simultaneously.

The chairman of the House Appropriations Committee decides to deny an Air Force request for $248,000,000 for spare parts for obsolescent aircraft.

In Spring Valley a popular hostess who last month contributed $5,000 to the Republican National Committee inspects a poll showing a rise in the popularity of the Democrats and writes a check for $5,000 payable to the Democratic National Committee.

BETWEEN 10 AND 11 A.M.

Fourteen reporters telephoning officers of the State Department are told that the men they want are in conference.

At the White House the Press Secretary calls in reporters to announce that the President, upon learning of the African head of state's tragic and untimely death in Scandinavia, has just cabled a message of condolence.

Two hoodlums subpoenaed before a House investigating committee refuse to testify, claiming their privilege against self-incrimination under the Fifth Amendment, and issue mimeographed statements accusing the committee of abusing human dignity and flouting the Constitution.

The senior senator from Mississippi, deciding that he is overdue for a speech denouncing the newest civil rights proposals, buzzes his secretary. "Get me my white-supremacy expert," he instructs her.

At the Burning Tree Club a three-star general and a senator step out of the shower. "I know how the Budget Bureau feels," the general argues, "but when you come right down to it, what the hell is another billion dollars more or less?"

BETWEEN 11 A.M. AND NOON

On the Senate floor the Majority Leader talks to reporters about the labor bill. "I never tell anyone how to vote," he is explaining. "On this one, every man will vote his conscience. We're going to be constructive. We're going to be positive. We're going to be responsible. We're going to do what's right for the country."

BETWEEN NOON AND 1 P.M.

The Secretary of the Treasury, lunching with the chairman of the Senate Appropriations Committee, explains that while he is an Administration team man 100 per cent, the Secretary of State's new international banking proposal smacks strongly to him of fiscal irresponsibility.

At the National Press Club bar an oil lobbyist meets the information officer of the Egyptian Embassy and asks: "Have you heard about the security-conscious secretary who left her Pentagon job to take a job with a bishop? She filed all his correspondence under two headings . . ."

BETWEEN 1 AND 2 P.M.

The senior senator from Wisconsin interrupts the debate on the labor bill to read "An Ode to the Old Dray-Horse," by a ten-year-old constituent.

A famous newspaper columnist meets secretly with the Majority Leader to learn what the Senate will do on the labor bill. The Majority Leader assumes his most confidential look. "We're going to be constructive," he confides.

Two governors arriving on the same flight at National Airport blame unemployment in their states upon the President.

Between 2 and 3 p.m.

The State Department correspondent for a weekly news magazine wins six dollars at poker in the Department's pressroom.

The President, while debating whether to retire a three-star general who has been going over his head to influential senators at the Burning Tree Club, receives a telephone call from the Vice-President. The Vice-President is worried. He suspects that the Senate Majority Leader is maneuvering him into a position where he will be forced to cast the tie-breaking vote on the labor bill. Perhaps, he suggests, this awkwardness could be avoided if the Budget Bureau would change its mind and agree to reactivate that old Air Force base in the Majority Leader's home state.

Between 3 and 4 p.m.

One hundred thousand government workers have a last cup of coffee to sharpen their wits for the rush-hour traffic.

The Senate debate on the labor bill is interrupted for the introduction of a delegation from a small Southeast Asian republic which is making a world peace tour.

BETWEEN 4 AND 5 P.M.

At his news conference the Secretary of State makes an ambiguous statement calculated to scare the French. The first news-agency bulletins misinterpret it to mean that the President is considering a break in diplomatic relations with India.

The Director of the Budget Bureau, calling upon the Secretary of the Treasury, voices the thought that has long been hanging unspoken between them: "Suppose— just suppose, mind you—that the President had the political courage just to abolish the Army altogether. . . ."

BETWEEN 5 AND 6 P.M.

The State Department press office calls a news conference to announce that, contrary to some interpretations, there is no consideration being given to breaking diplomatic relations with New Delhi.

The Senate debate on the labor bill is interrupted for a speech against the newest civil rights proposals by the senior senator from Mississippi.

Evening cocktail parties begin in all hotels, fifty-five embassies, and hundreds of private homes and apartments.

BETWEEN 6 AND 7 P.M.

Watching the early-evening news show on television, the President is flabbergasted by a film clip of the Secretary of State's ambiguous news-conference remarks about France. The President misconstrues them to mean that the Secretary is having an interdepartmental study made on the possibility of ceding Hawaii to Japan. A moment later the Secretary explains over the telephone that this is not the case at all.

The Senate debate on the labor bill is interrupted for a discussion of the relative merits of the rose and the marigold as the national floral emblem of the United States.

The President suggests to his wife that after Congress adjourns they vacation in Hawaii.

BETWEEN 7 AND 8 P.M.

The Vice-President and the Senate Majority Leader are photographed in friendly embrace at a cocktail party. "Say," asks the Vice-President, "have you heard about the security-conscious secretary who left her Pentagon job to take a job with a bishop?"

The second assistant to the deputy to the Assistant Secretary of State for Inter-American Affairs arrives home with his medal. "How did it go?" asks his wife. "The Assistant Secretary was there personally to make

the presentation," he says. "He mispronounced my
name."

The Senate debate on the labor bill is interrupted
while Administration critics take the floor to denounce
the Secretary of State's news conference statement,
which they interpret as a hint that the government is
about to recognize Communist China.

BETWEEN 8 P.M. AND 2 A.M.

A great Washington correspondent slips out of a
cocktail party after talking to three officers of the State
Department. He wires his paper an exclusive report on
"the inside story behind the Secretary's news-conference
gaffe today." What the Secretary's remarks really fore-
shadow, he reports, is nothing less than the dissolution of
the North Atlantic Treaty Organization.

After reading a Central Intelligence Agency report
on new missile installations in the Soviet Union, the
President plays a game of cribbage with his wife and
retires with a cowboy story.

The Senate, unable to muster a quorum, adjourns for
the day.

Four senators running for the presidency sit up with
their wives until all television stations go off for the
night and there is no more chance of seeing themselves
on the screen. Dropping off to sleep, each thinks: "I
know I'm the man for the job."

BETWEEN 2 AND 6 A.M.

The city sleeps, and each among its thousands of dreamers dreams of how brilliantly the country would be led if only he were the man in the White House.

The man in the White House dreams of six-guns and bunkhouses and of horseback living under prairie stars.

✳ *The Importance of Despair*

A FEW CAUTIONARY WORDS about the Washington temperament:

Finding contentment in Washington is easiest for those who really revel in a good crisis. During President Eisenhower's second term, the city furrowed its brow over three Quemoy-Matsu crises, two Suez crises, a flurry of Syrian crises, an Iraq crisis, a Lebanon crisis, a Cyprus crisis, and several Jordan crises, to cite only a few of the more remote.

In North Africa there was the Algerian crisis, which was only a fragment of what Washingtonians glumly called "the crisis of emerging Africa." In Europe there were French crises galore and a long-run Berlin crisis. Some of the French crises created crises for the North Atlantic Treaty Organization, and the perpetual Berlin crisis created periodic crises for the perpetual disarmament negotiations with Russia. In England there was a chronic balance-of-payments crisis.

For domestic worriers there was the economic crisis of 1957–8, and a perfectly delightful farm crisis—while multitudes elsewhere were living on near-starvation diets, Washington was spending billions to reduce food production. There was the segregation crisis with its concomitant crisis for the Supreme Court, and the leadership crisis, which had to do with the President's penchant for golf.

Looking toward Moscow, Washington discovered in quick succession a sputnik crisis, an education crisis, and a crisis in what is always called "the battle for men's minds."

The sputnik crisis revealed the existence of a defense crisis, giving the city an opportunity for some joyful agonizing over the problems of "the missile gap," "overkill," and "survivability." During lulls between crises, Washingtonians who had gone out into the country to look at television and the sinks of Las Vegas came back with somber reports that no one out there gave a healthy damn about the imminence of doomsday or the moral values that Mother used to teach. And so was born the crisis of the American moral fiber.

Having accepted great-power status, Washington had discovered trouble in a big way. Older capitals had known for a long time that in a world occupied by people there is always going to be plenty of trouble, and they are comparatively calm about it. They ration the number of crises they will tolerate over a year and reduce the others to the less frantic status of "questions," "problems," "situations," and "affairs."

Washington practices no such moderation. It is terribly excited about its new stature in international society and is hell-bent on turning it into a mission, which it conceives to be the salvation of all Hebraic-Hellenic civilization in its electronic manifestation. Thus, it runs a chronic case of high blood pressure. Wherever things are going badly, it is keen to flush a crisis. What it wants are not philosophers to administer sedatives, but men to match its miseries.

What must the visitor do to qualify as a worthy worrier? What he must not do is try to worry about the whole majestic field of troubles that Washington will spread before him. He should instead shop about and select one or two subjects about which he can brood like an expert.

In choosing, it should be remembered that, socially, Washington is a highly compartmentalized city and that the basis for most social groupings is a community of worries.

One's social locus is defined by the subjects he worries about. A man wishing to crack diplomatic society will not waste his time learning to worry about the farm problem, the Supreme Court, or domestic politics. If he wishes status with the political set, it will do him no good to cut into a conversation with a pungent comment on the ominous expansion of the Pathet Lao south of the Chinese frontier. First he will decide which segment of Washington society is for him; then he will specialize in the crises that absorb it.

Thus, if his is a truly fine capacity for alarm and if he also likes to see his name in the society columns, he will gravitate to foreign affairs. This is at once the most difficult and the easiest field to master. It offers such diversity of troubles that it is easy to find one that nobody else is worrying about and, so, to become an expert in quick order. However, one is expected to worry about foreign policy with an intensity demanded by no other group in Capital society. Let the halfhearted worrier therefore beware, for brooding on foreign affairs is a full-time and depressing task. The man lacking a Slavic capacity for despair will not go far.

For the irrepressible type, who cannot sit for hours scowling out the window, there is the noisy society of politicians. Their main worry is elemental ("Am I ahead or behind?"), but they also worry in a diffused, inattentive way about all the worries that all the other groups are worrying about intensely. Necessarily, this is a superficial, inexpert brand of worrying and requires no deep application. The society is also convivial, though not for the man who dislikes bourbon. (He can get by on scotch, but if he must have pink gin he will never get on with politicians.)

For the no-nonsense fellow who just wants the cold facts and the company of people who respect them, there are contending armies of economists eager to enlist him with honor if he can twist a bale of statistics into a passable theory. For more esoteric tastes there is the huge society of lawyers agonizing endlessly over the import of the three footnotes to the dissenting opinion in last week's Supreme Court ruling. And there is the labor group with its chronic terror of what Congress will do next. And the Pentagon set, tormented by the prospect of what will happen when there is no more money anywhere.

The choice is infinite. Although few can become expert in many of the yawning routes to doom, this never deters a Washingtonian from abusing the President whenever he fails to exhibit fully appreciative dismay about anything that is worrisome to anybody at any moment. The President is expected to be a fully rounded, Renaissance worrier. He is there to be criticized when caught without his worrying done.

The point to remember is that no one can last long in Washington who is not convinced that something some place is in hellish shape. Those who find it difficult being spooky for sustained periods will prefer Paris or Miami Beach.

3

The Society:

How to Put on the Dog without Pedigree

I F YOU WANT to get anything done in Washington, you must be in. In the know. In the swim. In the chips. In on the ground floor. In at the finish. In up to your ears.

People who are not in are worse than out. They are nobody. And when you are nobody in Washington, you do nobody any good and may soon be shipped back to clerical work in Elkhart.

This chapter, therefore, is dedicated to every American who arrives in Washington tormented by secret fears about his adequacy for fitting smoothly into the dazzling cosmopolitan society he has heard so much about. A certain amount of insecurity is inevitable, as on first coming to any alien place, but the adjustment, particularly for Americans, will be astonishingly easy once the basic customs and social structure are understood.

The difference between Washington and other cities is that in Washington everybody is in "society." Entertaining seethes just as relentlessly among the anonymous government clerks as among the million-dollar "hostesses" and in the most sumptuous embassies. "Society" as an exclusive group of the good snobby people scarcely exists here, except in vestigial form among a few old-line families quaintly called "cave dwellers." Status is entirely a factor of wealth and office. The Washingtonian moves up or down the social ladder according to the fluctuations of his bank account and his movements toward or away from the centers of power.

In brief, everybody can play, and does, and this makes it hard work. Whether Grandfather was a robber baron or a coal heaver, the players all start the race for the top from equal footing.

First, ten simple rules for avoiding trouble:

1. *Never keep the President of the United States waiting.*

2. *When addressing a congressman, say "Sir."* *If he happens to be a senator, fawn a little.*

3. *Do not abuse J. Edgar Hoover.*

28

4. *Quickly distinguish between friendly and hostile press people. Flatter the friendly as paragons of wisdom. Avoid the hostile.*

5. *Never invite the Chief Justice to a buffet supper and ask him how the Supreme Court intends to rule on that newsy case involving American Tel. & Tel.*

6. *Never wear yellow shoes in public unless you are a Southern senator.*

7. *Be careful about seduction. This is not Hollywood, and anyone caught exhibiting more interest in the libido than the ego is apt to be dismissed as a trifle ordinary.*

8. *Never be seen lunching alone. In Washington a man is judged by the people he lunches with. The lone luncher is a pariah.*

9. *Wait for the First Lady to ring you.*

10. *If you are a New Yorker, do not call attention to it. New York is under suspicion, especially among congressmen.*

If these injunctions are obeyed, the sky is the limit for the individual with a stout liver and the gall of a confidence man. Unlike the blood-line societies of other cities, the Washington social world cares little about breeding affidavits but a great deal about brass. Men are lionized not because they ride to hounds with dash, but because they have an air of importance, of being men who command events. The operative word here is "air."

They need not actually be men of importance; they need not actually command events. Seeming to is often enough to unlock all but the truly important liquor cabinets.

The reason for this is Washington's role as an international stopover for the influential. In such a society thousands upon thousands of strange faces may be important. In the confusion of the anonymous mighty, unnumbered fakers can pass unnoticed. Recently a hotel doorman confided to the local newspapers that it had been years since he had paid for a drink. At the dozens of cocktail parties held in hotel public rooms about the city, he had noticed, invitations were rarely collected and few of the guests knew one another. Thus, he explained, at the end of the day he had simply to change from doorman's uniform to business suit to stroll like a prince into whichever cocktail party struck his fancy. On rare occasions when someone asked for his invitation, he said, it was only necessary to smile and murmur that, unfortunately, it had been misplaced, and he was invariably passed to the hospitality of the bar. He had met the most interesting people, ambassadors, gangsters, senators, and famous actresses among them.

In a city where new important personages arrive every minute, the host who would avoid offense is necessarily exposed to harrowing risk. Betty Beale, society writer of *The Washington Star*, has recorded a story illustrating the problem for the highest society figures:

30

How to Put on the Dog

When Clark Clifford, one of Washington's most successful lawyer-politicians, received a call from his friend Senator Stuart Symington asking if he might send Dr. Edward Teller unaccompanied to a Clifford soiree that evening, the host readily agreed, though he had never met the celebrated nuclear scientist. When a short man with fierce black eyebrows and a long nose later appeared at the door, he was ushered in with the full honors due a hierarch of the scientific priesthood.

After bows to the awed guests, he suggested that they might like to hear what he could do at the piano. Enthralled by the prospect of seeing the great scientist entertain, the group gathered about and murmured admiringly as he rippled through "Laura" with professional ease.

While the piano tinkled, another guest appeared at the door. He was, he announced, Dr. Edward Teller. He was indeed. The gentleman at the keyboard was the professional pianist the Cliffords had hired for the evening.

This comedy of errors is one segment of the most disorderly, the most chaotic, the most democratic of all American "societies," a compound of celebrity hunters, name droppers, players of parlor games, marauding businessmen, politicians, freeloaders, quacks, crackpots, aspiring felons, stuffed shirts, fortune hunters, and expense-account millionaires. Entertaining is a perpetual condition of life. The limp handshake and the wilted joke are omnipresent; the hollow laugh, a requisite to survival; the hired butler, a symbol of affluence.

No other newspapers on earth devote so much space to "society" as Washington's. No other papers so thoroughly report a brisk exchange about the weather between a second assistant press secretary and the doorkeeper of the Senate barbershop upon meeting at a cocktail party for the retiring third secretary of the Cambodian Embassy. No other press palpitates at such extraordinary length over "society's" alarm at the rumor that the French ambassador may be recalled, thus ending the blooming career of a wife who had shown such chic at arranging mixed-nut centerpieces.

For all the commotion, however, it is a joyless "society" on the whole. Pervasive mythology about "hostesses" notwithstanding, the conventional Washington soiree offers scarcely more titillation than a convention of Methodist bishops. The stars of the social firmament, consisting mostly of transients, lack the tenure that creates the feuds which spice "society" life elsewhere. Most of them, being engaged in domestic or international politics, tend to be self-absorbed individuals whose communal leisure reflects the dusty narrowness of their interests. If it is lacking in the inbred mental invalids who disfigure more formal "societies," it also lacks the aristocratic spirits who enrich and outrage more class-conscious cities. It represents the democratic bourgeois triumph in its most advanced form, and the result is about what might be expected when Madame Verdurin has succeeded the Duchesse de Guermantes.

Still, the myths flourish, fertilized by the rich black prose of the popular magazines: The famous salons glittering with the conversational brilliance of the international set. Powerful hostesses changing the river bed of history with an invitation to dinner. Statesmen routinely transacting their business over cocktails. And so on.

Logic exposes the fraud. A man who empties the Senate when he rises to speak is clearly not going to become an Oscar Wilde by arriving at Mrs. Mesta's house. A cabinet officer who has not had an idea in a decade will not be transformed into a wit by an invitation from Gwendolyn Cafritz. The aging matrons who married great men when they were real estate salesmen are unlikely to visit parlors where their husbands will be exposed to international enchantresses. Men who have tricky business between them have eight telephones apiece and private offices in which to transact it, and are not likely to risk it under the influence of alcohol and in earshot of a gossip columnist.

✳ *The Urgency of Lunch*

THE WASHINGTON social day begins with a conference and builds with relentless speed to the first climax, lunch.

33

A Washington conference is much like a conference in any other city. Each man comes armed with an assortment of proposals cunningly contrived to make his colleagues sweat, and everyone kills a few hours dodging the hovering menace of responsibility. At the end, a committee is appointed.

When this ordeal ends, the conferee is free to start plotting his lunch. Only the callow will move frivolously at this stage, for here, as every Washington survivor instinctively knows, is the first crisis of the day, a test that can make or destroy the striver for status.

Remember, the important thing is seeming to be in the know. Unless you are one of the fortunates so powerful that you have boons to grant, being in the know is useless. People must *think* you are in the know!

How will they arrive at this conclusion? Certainly not by your telling them. If, for example, you are in elegant company and calmly state on your own authority that the President last week wrote a speech attacking Senator Survine but then burned it, you will arouse no one's interest. Your statement will probably be dismissed immediately as the fiction of a scheming brain. You may note in your listeners that impassive blinking of eyelids which means that they have recognized a lightweight.

But try dropping the same morsel in the following style: "I had lunch the other day with Jack McSweeney, who's helping to ghost the President's speeches. By the way, did you know that the President wrote a speech attacking Senator Survine and then burned it?"

This may not stop the party the first time it is tried, but it is certain to double your audience within the next eight seconds and provoke a few attempts to top you. These can easily be blasted now that the authenticity of your source is established. A supplementary clincher might go as follows: "I understand that the President was so furious about the mohair-subsidy bill that he took nine strokes on the fourth hole the other day."

Within forty-eight hours both of these items about the President will appear in famous metropolitan newspapers, solemnly garnished with explanations of their significance for next year's legislative program ("Prexy Reaches Breaking Point with Survine"; "Mohair Repealer Seen Certain"). Note that you have not actually said that Assistant Ghost McSweeney told you anything; you have merely stated that you had lunch with him the other day. In fact, you may have fabricated both items on the spur of a highball. No matter. From the audience viewpoint you have established yourself as a man in the know by the prefacing statement that you have lunched with McSweeney.

To pull this sort of coup regularly, it is obviously necessary to be seen lunching with McSweeney. It is foolhardy to be seen munching sandwiches at the People's drug counter or carrying a tray at Linda's Cafeteria. The ambitious will keep his lunch schedule filled with names suitable for dropping in the circle he wishes to conquer.

A good selection of lunch companions would include one member of the White House staff, a few Assistant Secretaries of State, a flag officer or two from the Pentagon, a scattering of senators, a famous pundit, a lawyer from the oil lobby, an economics professor on loan to the Treasury, three or four good ambassadors, and a mysterious friend from the Central Intelligence Agency. The last may be pure invention—possibly an old friend who rarely gets into town. The others can be lured to lunch on the pretext of extraordinary business to be discussed or on the strength of a casual introduction at any cocktail reception you may have crashed.

The chances are excellent that none will ever drop any indiscreet information, but this is irrelevant. Their presence across the lunch table will suffice to arm you with the authority needed to rise in Washington. Indeed, on the strength of the reputation that can be built, you may soon find these people calling *you* for lunch in the hope of profiting from being seen in your company. On days no one can be brought to table it is helpful, if one's employer or competitive colleagues are in earshot, to telephone the office of an unusually gaudy personage and tell his secretary that you would like to speak to her boss sometime at his convenience about lunching with you. She will promise to set up a telephone conversation for you—one of these days.

The Urgency of Lunch

The importance of lunch grows from the universal hunger for communication within a city where it is rapidly becoming impossible to understand anything that is said for public consumption. Lunch is not so much a meal as a forum where men from different agencies and businesses can meet, trade tiny fragments of information, and try to puzzle out, from their clandestinely bartered clues, what is going on.

Its intimacy breeds confidence and makes it immensely more important as a social function than the overpublicized cocktail circuit. Its protocol demands at least a token exchange of confidences about what is really happening inside the bureaucratic warrens along the river front. In a city where most official utterances are deliberately phrased to mislead, evade, or seduce, it is a reliable communication medium where a few men can at least try to explain honestly what the score is.

And so, thousands and thousands of telephone calls crisscross the city each morning in a groping for human contact away from the roar of the mimeograph machines and the hollow thunder of ghost-written inanities. Interestingly, the one place in town where lunch is nothing more than it is in any other city—a perfunctory gesture to the stomach—is the Capitol. There are various plausible explanations. The most persuasive is the unspeakable cuisine of the House and Senate dining rooms.

❋ Why the Cocktail Party

EXCEPT that it is cast on a scale that might have made
Cecil B. De Mille sigh, the celebrated Washington cocktail party is precisely like any other cocktail party. The
drinks are rarely well made. The air is inevitably fetid.
The guests cluster in bunches that swell, then subdivide
like reproducing amoebae. Conversations die in mid-
sentence as whole audiences peel away from the talker
to bore in on other groups like fighter planes on the attack.

The rug receives the orthodox per capita quantity of
cigarette ash and mashed cheese. The standard proportion of guests become tight, morose, fey, huffy, and
romantic, according to immutable natural law. An occasional adulterous rendezvous is projected, probably
to be canceled in the prosaic glare of daylight. Elderly
gentlemen behave foolishly. A young man insults his
boss.

The pattern is the same; only the scale is different.
In Washington it is done with a cast of thousands. Being
at a Washington cocktail party is like trying to walk into
Yankee Stadium with a martini in hand at the end of a
World Series game.

The guest list frequently seems to have been drawn
up by the Mad Hatter. The connoisseur of the cocktail
circuit will delight in noting the number of people he

meets whom he had thought dead for years. The widows of senators kicked out with the Ohio gang, cabinet officers forgotten since the Hoover administration, former assistant secretaries to Calvin Coolidge, wives of dead generals of the Grand Army of the Republic, lawyers who helped prepare the Teapot Dome prosecutions, European diplomats in disgrace since Munich. The whole society of the living dead can be rediscovered by faithful response to cocktail invitations.

The macabre variety of the guest list is explained by the cocktail party's omnibus character. It is the acknowledged device for working off uncertain obligations cheaply in massive social catharsis. While it is brutal on the furnishings, its compensations for the host are considerable. No guest really expects to be recognized on sight or to be listened to for more than a moment. Most can be counted on to leave by dinnertime. With a handshake and a rubber grin, the host can dispatch a year's accumulated social debts. Mysterious names that have lain in his files for half a century—because it is always better to entertain twenty nonentities than to risk offending one lion who may be hidden among them— can be had to the bar and sent away feeling that they still count.

Among the more common pretexts for cocktail parties are the farewell for some little-known embassy flunky, the hello for the new congressman, and the introduction for the big moneybags visiting from out of town. The most common victims are the embassy people, compelled by patriotism to accept every invitation; lower-drawer bureaucrats, delegated by their superiors to take on dirty work for the good of their agencies; and the press, driven by the tribal superstition of their clan that the way to get news in Washington is to live in an eternal soiree.

Except when they are guests of honor or intimate friends of the host, truly important nabobs are rarely to be found at the big cocktail party. Senators and representatives who count, justices of the Supreme Court, presidential cronies, civilized cabinet officers—in short, all the men every woman in Washington wants to grace her barbecue pit—have developed the defense of the movie stars. They pick their public appearances carefully, attend in a glum, dutiful way, and limit their social contacts to small groups of friends who, they know, will not claw the skin from their hands or expose them to confidence men and battalions of strange women.

The most awesome names in town may be inaccessible to the nationally celebrated "hostesses," but may drop in for dinner on an hour's notice at the house of an old friend with nothing to offer but quiet, congenial companionship.

✳ *Common Hostessing*

AFTER BRIEF EXPOSURE to Washington most wives develop early symptoms of what will eventually become a consuming passion to entertain. Publicly, every woman insists that she despises entertaining as a curse of Washington existence. This is not to be taken seriously. Usually it conceals an abiding envy of some acquaintance's poise against the candelabra and a single-minded determination to enter the lists.

The real queens of contemporary "hostessing" are mostly women who bought in with millions in middle life, but the typical young Washington matron is driven by the illusion that chic does more than millions can. Practice usually begins a few months after the young couple arrives and follows a predictable course. To try her hand, the wife may invite a few of her husband's colleagues for dinner. It will be an energetically informal buffet, usually consisting of shrimp mated with something in paste and meant to be eaten in sprawled attitudes among the living-room bric-a-brac. Afterward there will be charades.

The wife immediately notes that her living quarters are too small for proper entertaining, that her china is not up to inspection, that she lacks demitasse cups; but it normally takes one mortifying sit-down dinner with her husband's boss to clinch the decision: She sets out

41

to find a new house, "suitable for entertaining," and borrows on the insurance to acquire spode, silverware, damask, and a library on flower arranging.

At the same time she discovers the necessity of servants. Rented butlers, meat carvers, bartenders, and dishwashers begin to acquire a proprietary interest in the house. The husband wandering into his kitchen for a pre-party bracer is likely to incur the hostility of strange men sharpening meat cleavers or muttering Greek curses on the inadequacy of the refrigerator.

In the next stage, strolling musicians appear to harass the guests with accordion or guitar. Shrimp yields the table to imported pastes, unidentifiable meats smothered under wild rice, and huge quivering meringues supplied at astronomical prices by professional caterers. Names familiar to newspaper readers begin to appear, and the wife starts thinking about protocol. Now and then she will insist upon black tie.

In the mature stage, entertaining is formalized into what might be called "the ritual dinner." Because this is the type of after-dark occasion one is most likely to encounter, it will be dealt with in detail later. Here it is only necessary to note, that, in this stage, the hostess has become so inured to entertaining that her evening goes off with the automatic routine of a trip to the supermarket. This period is distinguished by the disappearance of the musicians, shrinkage in the staff of rented servants, a tendency in the husband, now graying, to yawn noticeably, and a sterile decency in everything done and said.

For most outings in Capital society, dress is relatively unimportant, especially for men. At the cocktail party, shabbiness is routine. Eyebrows would be lifted if a man appeared in shirt sleeves or without necktie, but toward muddy shoes, gravy stains, damp collar, crinkly lapel, and matted hair, the cocktail party is democratically tolerant.

The wild party is rare, though not scandalous. It normally occurs in the shrimp-buffet stage when the inexperienced wife falls hours behind schedule in the kitchen, with paralyzing effects upon guests left too long with the cocktail pitcher. To the veteran entertainee, this can be a delightful change in the drab nocturnal rounds.

These are the occasions when young matrons with finishing-school accents, leaning over a statesman, pour whiskey down the famous shirt front. And when the statesman, asked his opinion of a notorious colleague, replies in barnyard language. At one such affair not long ago, the tumult was interrupted by thunder from the stair well as the body of a pundit, tumbling end over end, rolled into view. "Heavens," said the gentleman's wife, "he's practicing falling down the steps backwards again." Sure enough, the journalist pulled himself erect, lumbered back up the stairs, and a moment later came tumbling down again. Backwards.

✳ *The Ritual Dinner*

WASHINGTONIANS go to dinner parties as gamblers go to race tracks. That is, not to have a good time, but because it is part of their way of making a living. They expect to meet someone who will be of use to them. They go with a systematic regularity that destroys any delight there could possibly be in the process. Because the dinner party is seldom a pleasant outing, but rather a duty that must be performed, they have evolved over the years rigid forms of behavior to which the guest is expected to conform.

First, he is expected to arrive punctually. Everyone wants to get on with it and end the day at a decent hour. The fashionably late arrival is not fashionable.

On arrival the guest may expect to be offered one drink. If he is fast and an extrovert, he may get a second. If he wishes to dine feeling no inhibitions, he is advised to take on coal at home beforehand.

Before his second drink is finished, he will be summoned to the table by a uniformed hired hand, probably rented for the occasion. There he will be placed between two of the opposite sex. He will be expected to chat with one through the soup and half of the entree, then turn and chat with the other through dessert. Small talk is preferred; the smaller the better.

Before coffee the hostess will rise to leave the room.

44

Males should rise with her. They should not leave the room with her. She is leading the ladies to a separate chamber, occasionally a boudoir, where they will continue their small talk, drink their coffee, and stay out of the men's way.

After the ladies' exit the host will offer cigars—sometimes after leading the males to yet another room—sigh expansively, then get down to the big talk. Brandy will be offered with the coffee. One is considered good form; two, when offered, bad taste.

After forty-five minutes the sexes reunite, frequently in still another room. At this point perhaps a drink of whiskey will be offered, perhaps a glass of water. Accepting the whiskey is occasionally approved for the more important male guests, provided they have had no brandy. Ladies will take water.

Shortly afterward eleven o'clock will strike. This is the signal, clearly understood by all, for the ladies to start searching for their gloves and murmuring to their husbands about the lateness of the hour. The guest of honor will leave first.

Then, if the host is the hardy or the unassured type, he will offer another round of drink. By no means should this be accepted! The offer must be answered by firmly setting aside what remains of any previous drink and insisting that departure be immediate.

The host and hostess will form a short line at the door. As the guest leaves he will express to the hostess his immense gratitude for a delightful evening. For the host, he should get off a final sally of wit, which has been stowed away just for this occasion.

On arrival home the lady guest will remove her girdle; the male, his necktie, coat, and shoes. They will then open a bottle of gin.

❋ Uncommon Hostessing

OF THE TWO attributes that make for distinction in Washington, office is the more potent, money the more permanent. Ladies planning to undertake hostessing on the grand scale should remember that they will be operating in a city of transients. Today's gods have a life expectancy of four years. Except in the case of certain human institutions with Southern accents at the Capitol, most of today's mighty titles will be preceded by "ex" before a struggling hostess can become entrenched. And no lion is quite so unexciting to the society columnists as an ex-lion. This season's prize catch is often next season's anonymous man.

The first rule for successful hostessing, then, is to beware of overcrowding the table with men marked for extinction. Cabinet officers and representatives are peculiarly vulnerable and should be cultivated in small lots, though cabinet men at the peak of their bloom are to be plucked without quibble. It is simply that one would be ill advised to try building a reputation exclusively on cabinet men. The President may have any of their heads in a bout of dyspepsia, and their average fame span is notoriously brief.

Presidents, of course, make the grandest guests of all, for no matter how churlish or uncultivated the man, he is the acknowledged traditional grandee of Washington society, and being on entertaining terms with him is enough to establish a hostess for years.

Perle Mesta ruled the field for years because of a friendship struck with a not particularly imposing senator named Truman when other famous ladies found him wanting in glamour. While Washington's front pages were still mourning the death of Franklin D. Roosevelt, the society pages were celebrating the ascendancy of Mrs. Mesta as the new queen of Washington society.

Justices of the Supreme Court are also excellent. Being only nine in number, they lend the table an aura of exclusiveness that senators cannot provide. Because they are beyond electoral revenge and may serve for life, they are fixed stars in a fluid social constellation and, once won to the sideboard, can be a mighty crutch for supporting a hostess through hard times. Regrettably, they are rarely gadabouts. Many eschew all grand society except the annual White House dinner in their honor, an obligation that cannot be avoided without creating headlines.

Certain ambassadors are splendid. The British and French ambassadors are always superb ornaments for any room. Washington has the turn-of-the-century heiress's envy of London and Parisian manners and goes as fluttery over these ambassadors as Zenith over a touring marquis. The Spanish ambassador is good, since Madrid usually caters shrewdly to American illusions about Castilian suavity.

The Latin-American ambassadors can be recommended unreservedly so long as the hostess has a pipeline into the State Department's protocol division for advice on how to handle them. No other group takes such a thoroughly professional view of entertaining and being entertained. Their code of what is and is not proper is as elaborate as the medieval tenets of chivalry. To seat one improperly is to invite a hemispheric crisis; this is a group that knows down to the last snail fork what its social prerogatives are, and the slightest misstep will be, at best, lamented as a swinish act of ill manners.

Senators are always acceptable, and those chasing the presidency, magnificent catches. The shrewd hostess will move quickly to cultivate a senator while he is still green, lost, and looking for the Washington he has read about in the "inside" columns by his home-town paper's representative to the Senate press gallery gin-rummy game. In these first days the senator is pliable. He needs someone to persuade him that he is important, for in the

Senate itself he is still being ordered around by clerks and inquiring about the location of the lavaboes. With luck the hostess may get in at the opening of a long or dazzling career. The chances are high that she will come up with nothing more than an assortment of dullards, but so long as her brood carry "Senator" before their names, their lack of any commendable quality will not tarnish the cachet which their title lends her salon.

Occasionally there will be a thoroughly distinguished senator who actually enjoys the nocturnal rounds. The most active in recent years has been Theodore Francis Green, of Rhode Island, who was still a full-time party man when he retired at the age of ninety-three. Green's engagements were so numerous that he carried a notebook to remind him where he was supposed to be at each of the evening hours. There is a classic story about the hostess who, noticing him checking it during her reception, asked: "Are you checking to find out where you go next?" "No," replied Green in his high-pitched, cultured voice. "I'm checking to see where I am now."

Representatives are a problem. Whereas the senator's six-year term and his natural lien on the headlines make him a solid investment, the representative's two-year term and his obscurity add up to a calculated risk. The Speaker of the House and the House Minority Leader, men whose tenure is as secure as any thirteenth-century baron's, rank among the elite and are to be sought with gusto. Beneath this imperial plane, however, the hostess may follow her inclinations, always remembering, of course, to keep an eye peeled for the man preparing to move over to the Senate.

The perspicacious hostess will also keep a city editor's eye on the comings and goings of the transient intellectuals renting their brains to the government. A nuclear physicist nowadays can be more chic than a Secretary of Defense. The Treasury may harbor professors with books on the best-seller list. The Justice Department, the Capitol, and the hundreds of private law offices may contain brilliant young attorneys who not only bring an impressive precision to the wispiest conversation but who may also turn up later in black robes or high office. Within the last few years, intellectuals have become quite distingué, though artists, philosophers, and poets remain unfashionable unless they are Russians on tour, or Robert Frost.

The hostess with just the right feel for Washington will also cultivate a few journalists. Here, sensitivity is everything, for the authentic knights of the hot dope and the crystal ball are few and the pretenders multitudinous. Generally speaking, syndicated columnists whose self-imposed cross is to point out the correct next move to the President, the Secretary of State, and the Pentagon may be expected to lure a respectful audience and to have their wisdom sounded even by senators. Those whose duty is to advise politicians and Congress are risky. Possibly given to heavy drink and pullman-car jokes, they should be approached gingerly until the hostess has had a look at their fingernails. Celebrities of the networks may be acceptable if seen regularly on sponsored news programs. Photographers and run-of-the-mine reporters are out of the question.

Military men are rather special. Like salad dressing, they should be chosen with great care for the effect they will give the total meal. The Joint Chiefs of Staff always make dandy, academy-trained guests, but the discreet hostess would not want to have, say, the Chief of Naval Operations on the evening she was entertaining a senator famous as the chief congressional lobbyist for the Air Force. Generally speaking, any officer with fewer than three stars will be reduced to mute suffering if the guest list includes an elected politician.

The one class that is absolutely never invited, under any conditions, is all other hostesses. Tradition demands that all other hostesses be cut dead on every occasion. Precisely why is not clear. It is one of those rules that Washingtonians accept as part of the life law, like never declining an invitation to the White House and never asking a senator in company for his opinion of the Metaphysical poets.

The tradition is respectably rooted in the historic feud between Peggy Eaton, the tavern-bred wife of Andrew Jackson's Secretary of War, and the highborn

Southern ladies grouped around Mrs. John C. Calhoun. The genteel group took the view that Peggy was a woman of unladylike predilections and, hence, beneath them. As in the clashes between gentility and influence ever since in Washington, the genteel were humiliated. Jackson, whose own social predilections were thoroughly anti-Charleston, put the power of the White House behind Peggy, and that settled it. Some claim that Mrs. Calhoun's refusal to bow cost her husband the presidency. Jackson's selection of Van Buren instead of Calhoun as his heir to the presidency, this argument goes, was influenced by his resentment toward the Calhouns' snubbing of Peggy while Van Buren was gallantly championing her.

In modern times the clash of hostesses has lost most of its political zest and continues only as an empty charade, profitable in publicity to all concerned but little more interesting intrinsically than a "feud" between television performers. Reams have been written about the refusal of Mrs. Cafritz and Mrs. Mesta to take tea together, and on one occasion when the two collided at a reception on neutral ground, the papers recorded it as breathlessly as a summit confrontation between East and West.

Having a coat of arms is very little help in becoming a society queen in Washington. How a woman sits a horse, plays the spinet, walks down a staircase, or holds a

52

glass has nothing to do with it. Wit, education, dress, working the Red Cross doughnut machine—all the things that distinguish the society woman in other cities are absolutely superfluous in Washington.

Here, the requisites are three: money, cleverness, and nerve. The basic equipment is one large house, decorated and furnished by the most lavish decorators and furnishers that money can buy, staffed with flunkies, and fitted with all the ware required to sustain an endless cycle of parties on a scale that might strain the resources of Conrad Hilton. At least one chauffeured limousine is *de rigueur,* and a private multi-engine airplane contributes to status.

Cunning must be exercised in placing the money where it will pay the best return in flossy guests. Money talks, according to the old saw; in Washington it screams. Politicians and their parties, always on the verge of bankruptcy, can be exceedingly courteous to the big campaign contributor and distressingly curt to those whose purses have been opened only to the opposition. It is not enough for the hostess to possess money; she must distribute it generously at campaign time.

The lady who places her bets well may collect an impressive list of acceptances when she mails her invitations to a new Administration. The loser can expect only gall. Nowadays, like the big corporations, hostesses hedge their bets by making clandestine contributions to both parties. It costs twice as much, but the payoff in guests is assured, regardless of which side wins.

Taking the plunge takes crust. Mailing out invitations by itself is rarely enough. Every trash basket in town holds a sheaf of handsomely engraved cards in unopened envelopes. A hostess without a reputation must get someone to build on, for when the quality of her service is still unknown, important names can nevertheless be lured if the evening is billed as a rite "in honor of" some other celebrity they want to meet.

One of the more common manuevers is to make contact with the person to be snared, say Senator Survine, and let him know that you have an especially gaudy eminence, say Jack McSweeney, on the dinner list. If Senator Survine takes the bait, the hostess then calls McSweeney and tells him he simply must come and meet Senator Survine. If Survine and McSweeney both bite, the hostess is in business. If McSweeney fails to show after Survine arrives? Well, hostessing is a pastime for women of resourcefulness and steel nerves. Ladies lacking in both should stick to being entertained.

✻ Addenda

FINALLY, three footnotes to dispose of questions nagging the practical-minded:

1. *Protocol*—This is a dismal science, like heraldry,

whose prophets specialize in such cataclysmic questions as who walks through a door first, how many cannons should be accorded the Foreign Minister of Zippity-Zap, and whether direct descendants of Pocahontas should curtsy to the Queen of England. The rules are more intricate and more easily broken than those of professional football. The State Department maintains a large department of professional advisers, which insists that it does not render opinions to private citizens. It will, if asked sweetly.

2. *White House Invitations*—Theoretically, the White House is the social apex of Washington. Invitations are tantamount to commands and are declined only on grounds of debilitating illness. The so-called White House social season is a short series of formal dinners and receptions, usually so circumscribed by protocol as to be utterly joyless except for those seeking material on which to fictionalize before their grandchildren. President Eisenhower found them so tiresome that some years he abolished them altogether and in others held them to the absolute minimum. No one should fear seeming gauche at the White House, for everyone is unsure of what he should do. Sometimes even the President. Eisenhower once learned from the papers that he had appalled his guests by appearing thirty minutes late to take the handshakes. A whole group of guests, the same evening, appalled the President by leaving tips for his cloakroom staff as they picked up their wraps.

3. *Will You Get By?*—Keep your tongue in your cheek, expect nothing more than a front seat at one of the human comedy's better side shows, and you will do fine. A few rare souls even have fun.

4

The White House

THE PRESIDENCY usually resists catalogue description. Where other offices of government are human institutions, the presidency is an institutionalized human. What the presidency may be at any given time depends upon the man who is President, and so its definition changes with the alternating temperaments of the men who pass the mantle from generation to generation.

The Constitution's definition helps a little. It vests the President with the executive power of government and requires him to carry out the country's laws and to "preserve, protect and defend the Constitution." It makes him Commander in Chief of the armed forces. It empowers him to make treaties and conduct foreign affairs. It requires him to appoint the Judiciary and the chief officers of the Executive Branch. It compels him to report to Congress from time to time and authorizes him to veto laws Congress wishes enacted.

At every point, however, the Constitution also opposes him with a political restraint. Though he is Commander in Chief, only Congress may declare war. Though he may make treaties, a bare one third of the Senate may repudiate them. Though he may appoint the Judiciary and the chief officers of the Executive Branch, a Senate majority may reject his appointments. Though he has the veto power, two thirds of the House and Senate may enact laws over his veto. Though his reports to Congress may urge methods for improving the Union and protecting it from peril, the House may refuse him the money to carry them out.

In this arid catalogue of powers and checks against power lies the taproot of the American political system. Out of it grow the great continuing clashes between men and philosophies which engage the national emotions and mark the country's progress. The serene phrase "preserve, protect and defend the Constitution" translates into Jackson's promise to hang John C. Calhoun for interposing state sovereignty against the federal authority, into Eisenhower's use of federal troops against Arkansas's defiance of the Supreme Court, or into the Civil War.

The treaty-making power and its check becomes the fateful fight between Wilson and Henry Cabot Lodge. The President's power as Commander in Chief, balanced against Congress's prerogative to declare war, becomes the ugly political battle over "Truman's war" in Korea. The appointive power, countered by the requirement of the Senate's "advice and consent," becomes the squalid personal quarrel between Lewis Strauss and a handful of senators or the slanderous abuse of Earl Warren before a Congressional committee hearing testimony on his fitness to be Chief Justice. The veto power becomes the Eightieth Congress's doomed struggle against the White House to regain for Congress its nineteenth-century ascendancy. The requirement that the President do his best to improve the state of the Union translates into the sublimated blackmail and bribery that is the everyday fare of political Washington.

But these examples barely begin to describe the office. The President is also the leader of his political party, though the Constitution recognizes neither parties nor party government. He is a molder of public opinion, another institution not mentioned by the Founders.

In company with the flag, he is the sacred symbol of the state, as the British sovereign is the unifying symbol of Britain and the Commonwealth. As such, he is more than Prime Minister; as head of government and party, he is more than King.

He is also, out of a modern necessity unforeseen by the Constitution, leader among other nation's leaders. And so, in the infinitely complicated political calculus of his office, he must compute the potential effect of his actions upon the domestic politics of the earth's other nations.

In his book *The American President*, Sidney Hyman sketches a picture of the routine administrative burden upon the modern President. In a typical year, he notes, George Washington signed 44 laws and one executive order, granted 9 pardons, made 65 appointments, and presided over a bureaucracy of 9 departments. Franklin Roosevelt in a typical year signed 408 laws and 315 executive orders. Truman in a typical year signed 9,500 pardons and made 25,000 appointments. The Hoover Commission computed that Truman was responsible for 9 cabinet departments, 104 "bureaus," 12 "sections," 108 "services," 51 "branches," 460 "offices," 631 "divisions," 19 "administrations," 6 "agencies," 16 "areas," 40 "boards," 6 "commands," 20 "commissions," 19 "corporations," 5 "groups," 10 "headquarters," 3 "authorities," and 263 other miscellaneous government organisms.

The Constitution prescribes only three qualifications for President. He must be at least thirty-five years old. He must have been a United States resident for at least fourteen years. And he must be "a natural born citizen." The Courts have never defined "a natural born citizen."

To these qualifications, political tradition has added others. For decades unwritten law required the President to be a white male Anglo-Saxon Protestant. Kennedy's election removes the disqualification of Catholics and Celts, but the country appears to be a good distance from qualifying Jews, atheists, Negroes, persons of Mediterranean and Slavic ancestry, and women—in other words, the great majority of the population.

The President is selected in a variety of ways: by automatic succession from the vice-presidency upon the President's death, by the choice of the House of Representatives, by winning a majority of 545 "electors." Electors are usually little-known political hacks selected in the leap-year presidential elections. Sometimes the electors' choice corresponds to the popular majority vote, as in the selection of Eisenhower, Franklin Roosevelt, and Hoover. Sometimes it is possible to win a majority of electors without winning a popular majority. None of the winners of five consecutive elections between 1876 and 1892, for example, had a popular majority.

Under the electoral system, each state's entire bloc of electors—crudely proportional in size to the state's population—usually goes to the candidate who wins a majority of the state's popular vote. Theoretically, a candidate could beat his closest opponent by only fifty votes and win all 545 electors. Because there are always several minor-party candidates, a close contest between the two main contenders may result in neither man's winning more than 50 per cent of the popular vote.

Presidents who won among the electors without winning a popular majority include Kennedy, Truman, Wilson twice, Cleveland twice, Benjamin Harrison, James Garfield, Lincoln, James Buchanan, Zachary Taylor, and James K. Polk.

John Quincy Adams was chosen by the House of Representatives after none of five candidates could muster a majority of electors. In the Hayes-Tilden election, Tilden won a popular majority over four other candidates but failed to get an electoral majority. In the resulting confusion Congress presented the White House to Hayes in return for a promise to withdraw Union occupation forces from the South.

History suggests that the wisdom of the popular majority may be questionable. Since 1828, when the first accurate statistics were kept, the President elected by the highest percentage of the popular vote was Warren G. Harding. He won 61.02 per cent of the total vote. The President elected with the smallest percentage had only 39.91 per cent of the total. He was Abraham Lincoln.

Presidents who have got to the White House by the vice-presidential succession are John Tyler, Millard Fillmore, Andrew Johnson, Chester A. Arthur, Theodore Roosevelt, Calvin Coolidge, and Truman.

Recapitulating the record, some curious facts emerge about the one office in the American government which is supposed to represent the will of the nation. Of the twenty-eight men who have occupied the White House since 1828, only eleven got there with the approval of a popular majority. They were Jackson, Van Buren, William Henry Harrison, Franklin Pierce, Grant, McKinley, Taft, Harding, Hoover, Franklin Roosevelt, and Eisenhower. In the 124 years between the elections of Van Buren and Kennedy, only two Democrats ever won the popular majority. They were Franklin Roosevelt, who did it four times, and that hapless anonymity, Franklin Pierce.

Since the Truman victory of 1948, it has become fashionable to argue that Presidents without a comfortable majority have no "mandate." This may be true. If so, Lincoln had no mandate for resisting Southern secession, Wilson had no mandate for his radical economic reforms, and Truman had no mandate for asserting American leadership of international resistance to Communist expansion.

The lesson seems obvious. Presidents do not have mandates; they have duties.

✳ *How to Be a Great President*

HOWEVER he gets to the White House, the new President quickly decides that being President is not enough.

He wants to be a great President. Here are a few suggestions for attaining greatness:

1. The first problem confronting every President, even before his Inauguration, is the selection of advisers. In forming the Cabinet, give the Treasury to a man like Alexander Hamilton and the State Department to a fellow like Thomas Jefferson.

2. The next test comes with the Inaugural Address. Here, something to lift the national spirit and capture the temper of the era is essential. If the nation seems unusually depressed, a sentence like "The only thing we have to fear is fear itself" would be just right. A literary flourish will also impress the historians. Use a few lines as appropriately graceful as "With malice toward none; with charity for all, with firmness in the right, as God gives us to see the right, let us strive to finish the work we are in."

3. Be a great democrat. The time to start is immediately after the Inauguration. Withdraw the police from the White House gates and let the public in for a reception. Let them track mud across the carpeting, smash the china, and smear cheese on the furniture. Historians will say that your fondness for the common man equaled Jackson's.

4. Is the country in economic distress? Try closing the banks for a few days. Bring in some professors and, in the first hundred days or so, have Congress pass bills the professors recommend. Look cheerful, jaunty, con-

fident. Carry the chin up and smoke through a cigarette holder pointed cockily upward. Go on television and radio and exude competence. Address the audience as "My friends" in a voice that convinces them that they really are your friends.

5. After the first few months detractors will begin to reappear, and the candidate for greatness must move with care, for now the presidential power is under challenge. Historians like to classify Presidents as good or bad according to whether they strengthened the presidential power, maintained it, or let it erode. At this point a sense of propriety is quintessential. Suppose a senator from Wisconsin, say, starts to terrorize the bureaucracy by using the congressional investigating power. If he is allowed to get away with it, history will deplore a presidential weakness. Study your opponent. Would he cut an ugly figure on television? If so, have someone arrange a long, entrancing Senate inquiry that will keep him on camera before the country for a good spell.

But what if the challenge comes from the Supreme Court? Suppose the Court begins declaring your professors' programs unconstitutional? One of the worst possible responses would be to try enlarging the Court by adding enough friendly new justices to give you a majority. Newspapers will denounce you, and history will report that you either suffered grave lapses of judgment or lacked respect for the Constitution.

6. Come up with a really new idea in foreign pol-

icy, something that can be summarized in about fourteen points and that contains a dramatic and durable idea comparable to the League of Nations.

7. Capture the public imagination by doing things that make people feel better. Say something exuberant like "Bully!" every once in a while. Go lion hunting in Africa. Get yourself cheered by a million Indians in New Delhi. Send the fleet around the world. Walk softly but carry a big stick.

8. Do something noble on the scale of the Marshall Plan.

9. Mold public opinion to your will with brilliant but homey analogies. If you want public support for giving the farm surplus to underfed peoples in Asia, call in the reporters and say something like "Now, if my cellar is stocked with food and my neighbor is starving . . ."

10. Be decisive in the right way at the right time. If something like the Louisiana Territory is for sale cheap, snap it up. When the opening occurs for a magnificent act like Emancipation, issue a proclamation. Extreme caution should be used, however, when under the impulse to fire a popular general.

11. When bargaining with other world leaders, outsmart them. Do not offer third parties concessions for joining you in a war that you have already won. Avoid attempts to negotiate the millennium with the Russians two weeks after they have caught your agents spying on them.

66

12. A few don'ts: Don't get off incisive letters to newspaper reviewers who write disparagingly of your kin's artistic, literary, or musical talents. Don't refer publicly to an unkind columnist as an "s.o.b." Don't appoint cabinet officers who will take bribes for giving the national resources to oil barons. When the country is threatened with civil warfare, don't leave it for the next President to handle. Don't appoint campaign contributors as ambassadors to Ceylon unless they know the name of Ceylon's Prime Minister. Don't get impeached.

13. Finally, cultivate luck, for without it greatness is beyond reach. What would Franklin Roosevelt's reputation be today if the Nazis had made the atomic bomb first? Suppose Lincoln's and James K. Polk's places in the order of Presidents had been reversed. Washington today might have a magnificent Polk Memorial, and adults might ask: "Who the hell was Abraham Lincoln?" What if McKinley had survived the assassin's bullet? Would Theodore Roosevelt have been buried in the anonymity of the vice-presidency? Or would he have gone on in 1912 to bury Professor Wilson in the catalogue of also-rans?

All this is hypothetical, merely a harmless time killer for the casual student of history. For the President, trying to chart the future course of history, each day demands answers to questions equally imponderable and usually far more fateful. On the quality of his responses hangs history's verdict on his stature. If he has the personal qualities his times demand, and if he has the luck, about all he can do to influence the verdict is to work so that the tombstone cutters may write, in Harry Truman's words: "He done his damnedest."

✳ The Survival Problem

THE WHITE HOUSE is a graceful, unpretentious structure situated on eighteen beautifully landscaped acres of choice downtown real estate in central Washington. As a residence it is more impressive than No. 10 Downing Street but not in a class with the Quirinal Palace or the Rashtrapati Bhavan.

"The White House" connotes more, however, than merely the house where the President lives. It is also used interchangeably to mean the man himself, the President, and the enduring institution that never dies and never loses at the polls, the presidency. The house is of little importance. The President may or may not be. What is important is the presidency and the means by which men have accommodated themselves to it and accommodated it to their wills.

These days the central problem of the presidency is implicit in the briefest recital of presidential responsibilities. Since the office was designed in the eighteenth century—for a small, loosely integrated country populated largely by farmers and insulated geographically from world politics—it has evolved into the most formidable concentration of power, outside Moscow, on earth.

In theory, its burdens are borne by one man. In fact, the work of the office requires hundreds of thousands of men, for the President must be expert in global and domestic economics, labor-management relations, the grand strategy of diplomacy and war, in business administration, tax theory, and desert irrigation.

He must be up to a snap decision about the wisdom of exploding the hydrogen bomb in anger, for no one else may order it done.

He must be a master politician, capable of blending warring factions of his own party into forms marketable at the polls. He must lead the partisan battle against the political enemy while retaining its affection for him as leader of the nation.

He must be an orator.

He must have divine insight into human nature, for it is also his duty to appoint hundreds of thousands of men to public office without knowing their faces or their names.

He must be a television personality, command the Army, Navy, Air Force, and Marines, and throw out the first ball when the baseball season begins. He must be a polished host, equally at east with royalty or workingmen.

He must accept prize watermelons with appropriate

rhetoric, declare days of prayer and patriotic weeks, send off condolences on newsworthy deaths, attend church regularly, correspond with the Russian dictator, and propose a bale of new laws each year and study each word of the finished product with the cunning of a lawyer equally adept in a police court or before the Supreme Bench.

He must have the prescience of Nostradamus, the indomitability of Winston Churchill, the subtlety of Machiavelli, the eloquence of Demosthenes, and the wisdom of Solomon. He must have the knowledge of the ages at his fingertips.

Obviously, if the President had to perform all the duties of the presidency, he would be a very busy man and the turnover rate among Presidents would rise quickly. Over the years a solution has evolved. This has been to create a lot of little Presidents, who absorb parts of the strain as it flows upward to the White House and who deflect all but the truly major worries before they reach the President.

For example, no one but the President himself can throw out the first baseball of the season, but the task of accepting the prize watermelon may be farmed out to a presidential assistant. The more routine chores are absorbed by the bureaucracy before they can reach the White House, though the President must always expect to take the responsibility for some flagrant stupidity or injustice committed anywhere among his subordinates.

Eisenhower, for example, was once surprised to hear from a newspaperman that a civil rights bill he had sent to Congress contained a provision paralleling an odious Reconstruction law. He promptly jettisoned that part of the bill.

Within the White House a staff system has evolved with variations to suit the temperament of each President. Ideally, the staff sees that the President gets the information he ought to have and is not burdened with more. This is not so simple as it looks, for one President's meat is another's poison. A professor's scribbled letter suggesting the feasibility of making an atomic bomb may be promptly put before him by a staff man who knows his professors, or shipped out to the bureaucracy for burial by a staff man who doesn't.

The general Washington law is that all staffs become overly protective. With Eisenhower overprotection reached the point of affliction. At one time John Sherman Cooper, one of the most distinguished senators of the President's own party, was unable to get an appointment with him to warn against the ill-fated Dixon-Yates power contract. Eisenhower's famous feud with Truman was accidentally intensified because someone, still unidentified, failed to notify Eisenhower that Truman wanted to talk to him on a Kansas City telephone. Truman was mortally offended because his call was never returned or acknowledged.

Excessive protection of the President probably

reached its peak with Sherman Adams, the former governor of New Hampshire, who sat for years like a cross between Cerberus and Jupiter in Eisenhower's antechamber. In an office called "The Assistant to the President"—since abolished by Kennedy in an attempt to break out of the insulation—Adams functioned as a demi-President in a way that first irritated and then outraged much of Washington.

With Eisenhower ensconced happily beyond criticism, Adams bore the brunt of all the criticism and abuse that no one dared to place upon the President-hero. He became a small legend. It was fashionable to say: "Adams has ice water where his blood should be." His supposedly iron soul was likened *ad nauseam* to the granite spine of his native state. A man of ruthless Puritan integrity, the cliché masters declared. His eyes were inevitably described as blue ice, his voice as a scalpel, his tongue as a whiplash. Secretaries, it was whispered, left his office in sobbing hysterics. Inside the White House, when he spoke on the phone important men called him "Sir" and knew he was finished with them when they heard his phone click, for he rarely bothered with the courtesy of a "Good-by." Or so it was said.

Washington accepted the thesis that Adams, not Eisenhower, directed the domestic and political activities of the White House. After Eisenhower's first grave illness cruel jokes began to circulate. "Good Lord!" went one. "Suppose Eisenhower should die and Nixon became

72

President!" "Worse," ran the punch line, "suppose Adams should die and Eisenhower became President!"

The end was not without poignance. What collapsed in the Goldfine investigation was the legend Adams himself had helped to create with his insistence on avoiding the limelight and friendships. The granite man, hauled out under the television lights, had his banal secret exposed: He was human. The revelation that he wore a gift coat of Bernard Goldfine's vicuña was as startling as the child's observation that the Emperor was naked, and the Adams legend dissolved in a gale of snickers. "I need him," Eisenhower pleaded while the public howled for his head, and finally, because the Republican party insisted, Eisenhower had to relinquish him.

The Adams story illustrates a lesson in understanding the modern White House. Wilson went through it with Colonel Edward House, Franklin Roosevelt with Harry Hopkins, Truman with General Harry Vaughan, Eisenhower with Adams. It is this: No matter how much Americans may adore a President, their native suspicion of great power makes them despise presidential advisers. They can select the President themselves, or so runs the illusion. (Actually, they merely pick between two men selected for them by professional politicians.) But they cannot prevent "a good man"—Eisenhower, say—from being seduced by some insidious fellow invited into the White House without public inspection.

This fear of a gray eminence slinking in through the

73

White House pantry and seizing the controls of state for God-knows-what sinister purpose is as common among the Washington sophisticates as with the American innocent.

Thus, Colonel House was depicted as a Svengali subtly pushing the gentle Wilson toward war, and Hopkins as a sadistic neurotic goading Franklin Roosevelt to "tax and tax" and "elect and elect." The attack on General Vaughan encouraged one to believe that he was directing wholesale perversion of government processes in order to amass food freezers. The history suggests that Americans would prefer their Presidents to forgo both friends and advisers.

Politically, it would be splendid if they could. The public being ever ready to swallow the thinnest piffle about some evil brain sheltered behind the President, the party out of power has traditionally exploited its gullibility by drawing the current Rasputin in the boldest possible lines.

Roosevelt's enemies hit hard on Hopkins's illnesses. A sick man, one was given to believe, who might therefore have dangerous impulses. General Vaughan was etched in the comic spirit, suggesting an unworthy atmosphere of low comedy in the White House, where, it was whispered, bourbon was actually drunk and "cronies" gambled for real money stakes.

Adams acquiesced in the sketch of his own caricature. He came determined to remain anonymous and not become an issue as Hopkins had. Ironically, this determination to avoid the sunlight assisted the creation of the Adams legend by planting a "mystery man" at the President's elbow.

Adams, Vaughan, Hopkins, House—all were manifestations of the humanity of the presidency. Some have called it the world's loneliest office. These men whom Presidents have needed and trusted and kept close despite public hostility testify to the loneliness of the place and to every President's need for the rare assistant who can share his mind and the rare friend who can sustain his trust.

Presidents will probably continue to pay high political prices, if necessary, for such men, for they ease the problem of human survival in a job that is probably too much for the best of men.

✳ *The Great Hagerty*

BECAUSE the presidency is a dynamic, constantly evolving office, civics texts on the subject are usually outdated before they leave the presses. No book now extant recognizes, for example, two unique contributions that President Eisenhower made to the office—mobility and James Campbell Hagerty.

As recently as Franklin Roosevelt's administration, being President compelled a man to sit it out year after year in the White House, with only occasional vacations and weekends out of town and, on rare occasions, a business trip abroad. Truman found time to vacation at Key West for fairly extended periods, but compared with what was to come, this was still the paleolithic age of the mobile presidency.

Eisenhower turned the job into the most powerful permanent floating office in history. For long periods you hardly knew where "the White House" would be from one day to the next. For two months it might be in Denver. Then it would move to Gettysburg or be off to Palm Springs. The Little Rock school trouble was dealt with from Newport, Rhode Island. The White House was in Thomasville, Georgia, during a furor about arms shipments to Saudi Arabia, and in Augusta, Georgia, on the average of two seasons per year. It was stopping over in Monterey, California, when it revealed the sites of the Soviet Union's hitherto secret nuclear testing grounds. And in the latter days of Eisenhower's term it was temporarily housed in Rome, Ankara, Karachi, Kabul, New Delhi, Tehran, Athens, sundry warships at sea, Tunis, Casablanca, Paris, London, Bonn, Seoul, Manila, Rio de Janeiro, Buenos Aires, and Brasilia.

What made it possible for Eisenhower to keep the presidency in a suitcase was the full flowering of the technological age and the acumen of his constant traveling companion, Jim Hagerty. The one provided fast courier planes, instant telephone and wire communications, and all the trappings that make it possible nowadays to work by remote control. Hagerty provided the genius necessary to keep the presidency in the public eye after it had passed beyond the Washington horizon.

In years on the road, no matter how remote or idle the President, it was a rare day when the resourceful Hagerty failed to produce some morsel of "news" to keep alive the idea that being President was a full-time job. His severest tests were met in the old railroad depot at Fraser, Colorado.

Before his heart attack Eisenhower liked to retreat for brief fishing trips each summer to the ranch of a friendly Denver banker high on the Continental Divide in the Rockies. For days at a time, while nothing happened but fishing, Hagerty would come down to the depot, sit by the potbellied stove, and ladle out a thin gruel of "news" to the dozen or so reporters seeking to justify their expense accounts.

Hagerty gave them the President's own recipe for vegetable soup. Bulletins were wired that the preparation of this famous concoction, which took twenty-four hours to make, had begun, then that the soup was nearing the desired thickness, finally that it was completed and had been consumed.

When the soup story palled, Hagerty produced reports on the fishing or revealed that the President had taken pistol practice at knotholes or was embarked on an oil painting of nearby peaks or had been "in touch with" some cabinet officer in Washington about matters on Page One.

Hagerty found the reporters eager to accept such trifles and was occasionally abused for showing up empty-handed. The editor's habit of seeing a White House story in his paper every day is so ingrained that many White House correspondents would have become former White House correspondents had they been content to wire the only news: "Ike loafing. Me too. Unfiling this week."

Hagerty, in these wastelands of tedium, not only did every future President a service by keeping the editors addicted to the habit but proved forever the maxim that almost anything at all about the President is news.

There was one memorable exception. It occurred one day when the soup story had run dry and it seemed that even Hagerty could not dredge a fragment of news. That afternoon, however, he arrived at the depot in considerable agitation, took his customary seat, and with the pleased look that meant he was about to distribute something exquisite, announced that the President only minutes before had signed a treaty. Pencils worked as Wayne Hawks, the White House records chief, produced a huge beribboned parchment scroll.

Hagerty beamed as Hawks unfurled the parchment. The reporters' expressions changed to dismay as they read through it and saw their visions of a Page One diplo-

78

matic story evaporate. What the President had done was to affix his signature to a routine treaty, signed months before by the negotiators, providing for a continuation of telephone communications between the United States and a small Central American republic.

The vastness of this triviality produced by Hagerty's mobile news factory was so overwhelming that the reporters began to laugh. Hagerty frowned and assumed his hurt-and-angry expression, but as the laughter continued to rise, his grim façade cracked and he joined in. Hawks rolled up the treaty and carried it out, a monument to the truth that a White House Press Secretary may make the papers with no news but cannot do it with old no news.

Hagerty's most glorious triumphs at Fraser were the rare days he passed the newsmen through the gates of Eisenhower's retreat into the presidential presence. This was no piddling accomplishment, for Eisenhower had not felt jolly toward reporters since a poll of correspondents on his 1952 campaign train showed that a lop-sided majority favored the election of Adlai Stevenson.

In 1954, however, Hagerty scored a coup by getting his flock inside while Eisenhower was host to Herbert Hoover. A few days earlier the press had reported that the President while fishing had caught over the legal limit, and Eisenhower's private reaction suggested that he thought freedom of the press had been pushed beyond endurance. The meeting inside the President's retreat was remarkable chiefly for Hoover's observations on the evolution of the presidency.

Sternly and with a good deal of feeling, he told the journalist-trespassers: "Thirty years ago we used to believe that there were only two occasions on which the American people would protect the privacy of the President. That was at prayer and fishing." Turning to Eisenhower, he said: "I now detect that you have lost that last one. The press no longer regards the privacy of the President when he's fishing. That is one of the degenerations of the last thirty years."

Mr. Hoover's plaint about the loss of presidential privacy illuminates the difference between the pre-Hagerty White House and the post-Hagerty model inherited by his Democratic successor, Pierre Salinger. Under Hagerty, constantly pumping the White House for news, Eisenhower enjoyed the most sustained press support of any President in history. Hoover, by contrast, started with an admiring press and turned it into an enemy. One of the turning points, ironically, was a fishing trip on the Rapidan River, where Hoover's privacy was rigorously maintained by a Marine guard. Shut off from contact with him, the reporters learned one day that he had hurriedly broken camp and headed back to Washington. They raced back behind him and turned in accounts of the President's surprise trip to town made at unusually high speed. His speed was computed from the time it had taken him to cover the mileage, but the simplicity of this source was apparently beyond Hoover, who ordered an investigation to find out who in his party had betrayed his speed to the papers.

With Hagerty, the nonpareil of the press office, Hoover might at least have cut his losses, as Hagerty enabled Eisenhower to cut his by keeping up a steady if thin trickle of presidential news during long vacation idyls. In Washington there was a great deal of overdrawn speculation that Hagerty was also a silent but influential shaper of high policy in the White House. This is to be taken with skepticism. Hagerty's enduring contribution to the White House was his demonstration of how to exploit the weaknesses of the American newsgathering system for the promotion of his boss.

A former newspaperman himself (he had learned the trade on *The New York Times*), he knew the weak spots and was quick to uncover television's. If editors demand a presidential story per day, it follows that reporters will be found to satisfy them one way or the other. On days when there is no news, they will poke around darkened rooms, look under the carpet, or start staring at the west wall and adding two and two in news stories. When that sort of thing happens, the White House is in trouble.

Hagerty prevented this by seeing to it that there was rarely a newsless day. If there was no news, he made a little. During the President's convalescence from coronary thrombosis in Denver, when the country might logically have assumed that Eisenhower was not functioning as head of the state, the device was used of flying in cabinet officers and sending them into the presidential sickroom to "confer."

After each man left Fitzsimons Army Hospital he was escorted by Hagerty back to press headquarters at Lowry Air Force Base and put through a news-conference routine. Inevitably the visitor would begin by announcing that he had been amazed by the President's vigorous, healthy appearance. He would go on to report that he had discussed with the President details of some new program then being mulled over by bureaucrats back in Washington. John Foster Dulles said he had got final advice on a meeting of Foreign Ministers that was about to take place. Other topics that the visitors insisted they had discussed with the President suggested that the doctors were taking a relaxed view of coronary thrombosis.

Herbert Brownell, the Attorney General, told of a chat about new prison construction. James Mitchell, Secretary of Labor, talked about the "good strike record" that year. George M. Humphrey, Secretary of the Treasury, said he had told the President that he hoped for a balanced budget.

Despite the resulting impression that Eisenhower had been on top of his job during those weeks in the hospital, the President himself later gave an authentic idea of how

isolated he had actually been. Shortly after his convalescence, he told his news conference that he had been
so cut off from public affairs that he was not even told
that the stock market had suffered its worst break since
1929 at news of his illness.

Because the tradition of the American newspaper
compels it to report with straight face whatever is said
by anyone in high office, it was unable to suggest any
element of charade in the parade of cabinet officers to
Denver. And so, in a sense, the press was seduced with
its own morality.

Future White House Press Secretaries will also
study another Hagerty technique, the art of muscling
the White House in on the good news story. While Eisenhower vacationed at Monterey in 1956, for example,
Hagerty had the President announce that new Russian
nuclear tests had just been detected and that the Soviet
testing grounds had been located near the Arctic Circle
and in south-central Siberia. Normally such news is announced by the Atomic Energy Commission in Washington, but at a time when there was no presidential
news but golf, Hagerty snatched it for the White
House.

In 1958, when earth satellites were still good for a
banner headline, the White House reporters consulted
Hagerty one day about how the news would be released if an Army satellite fired that morning should go
successfully into orbit.

The news of the first successful satellite had been released by the White House at Augusta, where the President was golfing. The reporters wanted to know if the White House would also announce the results of the second attempt. "If it is in orbit," Hagerty explained, "we would have an announcement." Suppose it did not orbit successfully? Would the announcement of the failure come from the White House? "No," Hagerty replied. The satellite did not orbit successfully and the White House did not have Eisenhower's name attached to headlines of failure.

This recitation does not exhaust Hagerty's resources. Knowing that troublemaking news almost always comes from a chat between some lesser figure of government and a reporter, he began by closing down communications between the White House staff and the press. All information, he made clear, was to be funneled through his office. Reporters seeking interviews with White House workers were told to get clearance from Hagerty. Interviewing one under these circumstances was like having a tête-à-tête with a mollusk.

Eventually the White House reporters all but gave up and settled into the leather cushions of their sealed-off lobby, like courtiers in solitude, to doze, consume paperback novels, or just breathe quietly until Hagerty summoned them for a spoon-feeding.

✻ *The Satisfying Misery*

BEING PRESIDENT IS, in many ways, the nicest job in Washington. The salary, though not princely compared with what a successful crooner can earn, is $100,000 a year, and expense allowances are generous. The White House is rent-free, complete with limousines. The Air Force places an armada of aircraft, from helicopters to four-engine jet liners, at the President's disposal. The Navy offers a variety of ships to suit the President's tastes in cruises.

A President also meets a lot of interesting people, many of whom are not accessible to even the most successful crooners. He may see his name in the papers every day, watch films of himself in action on television and movie screens, have himself psychoanalyzed regularly in the press, and call special sessions of Congress.

When he goes in the streets he requires a special bodyguard to protect him from idolaters. He is welcome in the homes of the rich and fawned upon by the masses. Fleets and armies are his to command. His name is one of the world's household words. He may fire generals who irritate him and pardon the condemned. His every word is magnified, reproduced, circulated, and studied with a respect suggesting that his wisdom transcends Plato's.

Here, surely, is a job to satisfy the most energetic

craving for fulfillment. Yet any man about to assume the office would err seriously if he failed to cultivate a mournful countenance for use shortly after his Inauguration whenever he discusses his work publicly. He may, in fact, love it, but he should never admit it.

The last man who did was Theodore Roosevelt. "I will confess to you confidentially that I like the job," he wrote as his term ended. When he tried to win it back in 1912, Wilson was elected.

For public consumption the President is expected to make frequent statements suggesting that being in the White House is a hellish imposition. This not only has the sanction of tradition but also suggests a magnificent selflessness in the man. A typical tenant's reference came from Warren G. Harding after his first term in residence. "The White House," he said, "is a prison."

Presidents Truman and Eisenhower, among others, echoed the sentiment. Truman pronounced it a "jail." Eisenhower was subtler. He fostered the notion that merely requiring the President to live anywhere in the District of Columbia was inhumane. Campaigning in the West in 1954, he told audience after audience that, by golly, it was good to get out of Washington and see "Americans" again. This not only left his audiences feeling superior but, by suggesting that Americans were not to be seen in Washington, warmed them to Eisenhower as a man willing to put down among aliens in order to champion the American way. Here, they were invited to believe, was a rare and noble creature, an American in Washington.

Despite the custom of complaining about living in the White House, the hordes clamoring to move in have diminished none over the decades, and the prisoners, for all their groaning, rarely leave without a shove when the gates are opened every four years.

The only exceptions in modern times have been Truman and Coolidge. In neither case is the record entirely convincing. Though constitutionally entitled to run again in 1952, Truman had already served nearly eight years, almost two full terms. Refusing to run in 1952, he was returning to the old tradition of refusing a third.

In 1948 he had fought his party leaders to remain in the White House despite their pleas for him to take his freedom and give way to a candidate who could beat Thomas E. Dewey.

Coolidge's case was the more exceptional. Reporters vacationing with him in the Black Hills were one day handed slips of paper bearing the words: "I do not choose to run for President in 1928." The Republican party interpreted this cryptic message to mean that he would not run for a second term, and it promptly turned to another candidate.

Historians have mused ever since over the theory that Coolidge really did want to run but was betrayed by his economical Vermont prose. What his lean sentence really meant, this theory has it, was: "It is immodest to ask for the job again. Persuade me." In any event, the Republicans did not choose to persuade him. Once they had accepted his statement as a resignation there was nothing Coolidge could do in good grace but leave quietly.

Franklin Roosevelt, on the other hand, simply refused ever to be put out. When the delicate question of a third term arose, he left it open until the Democratic Convention met in Chicago. There was none of Coolidge's cool ambiguity when he decided to strike. The delegates got the cue that he was running again from the convention loudspeakers, which mysteriously began booming an appeal for "The Champ." Investigation revealed that the voice that started the stampede belonged to Chicago's chief of sewers, who had commandeered the amplifying system. To this day Republicans declare that Franklin Roosevelt accepted the third-term nomination in response to "the voice from the sewers."

In this day of positive thinking, it is considered cynical to suggest that, all their protests notwithstanding, men enjoy being President and moan publicly about the misery of it only because precedent demands it. Even without the material gratifications, it is hard to understand why a normal man should not enjoy it. If it is not indecent for a man to relish the trivial authority that goes with the directorship of a motorcar company, a television network, or a trade-union federation, why should the joy of testing himself against challenge become unworthy when the test is truly homeric?

To be sure, the responsibilities are awesome and the avenues to catastrophe broad enough to inspire the most zealous with a sense of modesty. But for the man who yearns for immortality, it is also the high road to status with Caesar and Lincoln. To protest that there is no pleasure in such an estate is unconvincing.

Such protests as have come from Presidents Truman and Eisenhower (Harding admittedly had a case) are not to be taken seriously. They should be dismissed as sops to an honored custom, in a class with the screen goddess's complaints that her fans will not let her alone in night clubs. Nevertheless, Mr. Kennedy and his successors will doubtless want to perpetuate the custom, and may even do so with great conviction in some of the moments ahead.

5

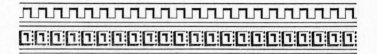

The President's
2,500,000 Right Arms

Following is a random sampling of events that occurred within the bureaucracy during the period 1957–9:

1. After a protest from Representative Donald E. Tewes, of Wisconsin, the Department of Justice agreed to revise its handbook *How to Cook in Jail* to include more recipes calling for butter. The decision was reached after Tewes complained that ninety-four recipes in the booklet required oleomargarine while only one mentioned butter, the glory of his native state.

2. The State Department decided against a showing of *South Pacific* at the Brussels Fair on the ground that its subplot, an interracial romance between a white man and an Asian girl, would annoy Southern senators. After several other Broadway successes, including works by Tennessee Williams and Arthur Miller, were rejected on the ground that they would irritate this or that pressure group, one diplomat suggested *Waiting for Godot*. Since no one could understand it, he argued, no one could possibly be offended.

3. In a memorandum, the Defense Department cautioned itself against divulging that monkeys were being shot into space in rocket research. Cannily the military revealed that "primates" were being fired off, but refused to talk when asked if "primates" meant monkeys. A man with a loose tongue revealed that they were monkeys, all right, but that the Pentagon feared the publicity would arouse Asian monkey cultists.

4. After deliberation the National Labor Relations Board refused to act against an employer who had fired a washing-machine repairman for leaving a customer the following note:

"Here is the grinding noise. Had to dismantle the washer to get it out. Machine otherwise okay. Suggest you check thoroughly for bobby pins before washing your hair in this washer. Also keep your mouth closed as the motion of the agitator has been known to dislodge dentures while beating the head back and forth. Also remove your glasses and keep your eyes closed. Your bill will be $6."

5. In the press office at the Pentagon someone posted a sign reading: "If the boss calls, get his name."

6. A veteran employee of the Department of Health, Education, and Welfare revealed that she kept in stock two form letters for replying promptly to the periodic recommendations of business-management consultants for increasing the efficiency of her office. The first read: "To effectuate the recommendations of this report will require an amendment to the Constitution of the United States." The second read: "To effectuate the recommendations of this report will require the repeal or amendment of the law establishing this program."

7. The Office of Civil and Defense Mobilization opened a quiet campaign to persuade the public to quit calling it O.D.C.M. and start calling it O.C.D.M.

8. The Labor Department selected "radiation purple" as the "theme color" for the meeting of the President's Conference on Occupation Safety.

9. The Army issued AR 380-40 (C 1) announcing that AR 380-40 had been amended so that all references to KAG-1/TSEC and KAG-2/TSEC would henceforth read KAG-1A/TSEC and KAG-2A/TSEC, respectively.

10. Reviewing a ghost-written campaign speech that Eisenhower was due to deliver, members of the White House staff split over the question of leaving in a

passage denouncing the Democrats as "gloomdogglers."
The ghost writer's wife, Mrs. Malcolm Moos, interrupted the conference to call for her husband. Someone
asked what she thought of the word. It sounded "cute,"
she said. The next day in Baltimore the President denounced the Democrats as "gloomdogglers."

11. The State Department, planning its new building, contracted for a $40,000 incinerator for burning
"classified trash," waste paper too sensitive to be
chanced a passage through janitorial hands. The blueprints included a system of chutes for conveying the
"classified trash" from loyalty-screened stenographers
directly to the flames.

12. The legend "White House Mess" was ordered
removed from matchbook covers distributed in the mess
operated by the Navy in the White House.

13. A two-hundred-pound panda residing in Peiping
was denied admission to the United States by the State
Department. State, disappointing domestic zoo men, invoked its taboo against trade with Communist China,
ruling that the panda's admission would imperil the national security.

14. After two senators received complaints that the
American Pavilion at the Brussels Fair contained en-
gravings of a semi-nude woman watching a group of
savages turn a human carcass on a spit, the Director of
the United States Information Agency was flown to Bel-
gium to investigate and report to the President.

15. The State Department accepted informal complaints from Paris after the American press carried reports of a political falling out between President De Gaulle and his cook. State was advised that the cook was actually devoted to De Gaulle and had been terribly upset by the incorrect American reporting, thereby jeopardizing the tranquillity of the General's kitchen.

This catalogue could be expanded, but the samples suffice to convey the flavor of day-to-day life within the government labyrinth. Some will be impressed by the gross triviality of it. Is it not outrageous that men supported by tax revenues should have to spend their hours debating the wisdom of calling Democrats "gloomdogglers," guarding the national security against pandas, and devising tricky synonyms for "monkey"? Why should the taxpayer support such nonsense?

The answer is that the American, though sulking about a profligate bureaucracy, insists upon it. The Wisconsin dairyman, embattled with the oleomargarine interests, demands the government's help. So does the laborer fired for yielding momentarily to picayune impulse. The man who is shocked by an American exhibit in Brussels expects action when he complains to his senator. It requires money and men to get it for him. When Uncle Sam is expected to play big brother to 180,000,-000 people, he obviously needs assistants, and plenty of them.

Plenty of them he has. In 1800 the federal payroll consisted of about 130 clerks. The State Department staff was five men. There was not even an office for the Justice Department. The Attorney General paid for his own quarters and staff out of pocket.

From these spare beginnings grew today's federal behemoth, which consists of approximately 2,500,000 employees, exclusive of the armed forces. Concentrated in a single place the bureaucracy would create a metropolis comparable in size to metropolitan Boston, San Francisco, Pittsburgh, or St. Louis. Laid in a straight line, head to toe, its members would form a human bridge extending from the base of the Washington Monument to the Golden Gate.

They are not concentrated in one place, of course, or prostrate in a transcontinental line, but diffused around the planet. Washington is home for about 200,-000. Even on this scale, it is hard for the mind to grasp.

Imagine a single building three times the size of the Empire State Building, housing 30,000 people with 3,000 clocks to watch, providing every service required to support life comfortably—restaurants, cafeterias, department stores, clothing shops, drugstores, medical and dental offices, libraries, telegraph offices, gymnasiums and swimming pools, bookshops, temples of worship. This is the Pentagon, a mere nook in the government warren. Its denizens, housed along seventeen and a half miles of

stone corridors, annually dispose of $40,000,000,000. A
man on a $100-a-week salary would have to work
7,692,308 years to earn $40,000,000,000.

The Pentagon, home of the Department of Defense,
is only a fraction of the total. There are the nine other
cabinet departments—State, Treasury, Post Office, Justice, Agriculture, Commerce, Labor, Interior, and
Health, Education, and Welfare.

And the Atomic Energy Commission, the National
Aeronautics and Space Agency, the Civil Service Commission, the Civil Rights Commission, the Tariff Commission.

The White House has spawned its own little constellation: the Budget Bureau, the National Security Council, the Office of Civil and Defense Mobilization, not to
mention a legion of special presidential committees.

Another system of agencies revolves around the twin
suns of the Treasury and State Department: the International Cooperation Administration, dispenser of foreign aid; the United States Information Agency, dispenser of propaganda; the Export-Import Bank, making
hard loans to foreign countries; the Development Loan
Fund, making soft loans to foreign countries; the Inter-
American Development Association, making soft loans
to Latin countries; and so on. "A bank a day keeps the
Communists away" is the slogan of the age.

There are the police departments: the Central Intelligence Agency, the Treasury's Secret Service, the Jus-

tice Department's Federal Bureau of Investigation, the Pentagon's offices of Military and Naval Intelligence. There is the National Security Agency, maker and breaker of cryptographic codes. There is each agency's internal-security agency, constantly checking the habits, proclivities, and thoughts of the parent agency's employees.

There are the quasi-judicial regulatory agencies lying in the no man's land between White House and Congress, theoretically keeping a stern federal eye on entrepreneurs and industrialists: the Securities and Exchange Commission, the Federal Trade and Power commissions, the Interstate Commerce Commission, the Federal Communications Commission, and the Civil Aeronautics Board, which is not to be confused with the Civil Aeronautics Authority or the Federal Aviation Agency.

Have we overlooked the Advisory Committee on Weather Control?

Or the Air Coordinating Committee, the Airways Modernization Board, the American Battle Monuments Commission, or the Arlington Memorial Amphitheater Commission?

The end is not yet, though you beg for mercy.

There is the whole galaxy of agencies dabbling in finance of one sort or another. The Federal Reserve Board, the Federal Deposit Insurance Corporation, the Federal Home Loan Bank Board, the Housing and

Home Finance Agency, the Federal Housing Administration, and the Federal National Mortgage Association, always called "Fanny May."

What of the Farm Credit Corporation? Of the Commodity Credit Corporation?

The Subversive Activities Control Board. The Renegotiation Board. The President's Committee on Youth Fitness. The Small Business Administration. The Tennessee Valley Authority.

The Veterans' Administration.

The St. Lawrence Seaway Development Corporation.

The Foreign Claims Settlement Commission.

The National Labor Relations Board.

The National Mediation Board and the National Science Foundation. The Indian Claims Commission and the Committee on Purchases of Blind-Made Products.

Abandon the catalogue and consider the people—the toilers who man the in baskets and the out baskets. These are the solid middle-class backbone of Washington's population, providing the city with its biggest payroll. They are the people one is most likely to stand beside in the bus or collide with in the supermarket. Who are they?

The deputy chief of protocol at the State Department. The second assistant secretary to the Assistant Secretary of Defense for Public Information. The chef of the General Officers' Dining Room in the Pentagon. The chauffeur of the Secretary of the Treasury.

98

The stenographer of the secretary of the assistant to the general manager of the Atomic Energy Commission. The second deputy to the public affairs officer of the Division of Middle Eastern Affairs of the State Department. The undercover agent in charge of formenting revolutions for the Central Intelligence Agency. The security officer of the Department of Labor.

The ghost writer of the President's ghost writer. The deputy to the second assistant secretary in charge of stencils of the General Services Administration. The assistant to the night watchman of the National Archives. The press officer of the safety officer of the Civil Aeronautics Board. The chief elevator operator of the Washington Monument.

The chief herpetologist of the National Zoo. The assistant to the chief of the African Division of the Division of Research and Intelligence at the State Department. The head door opener of the presidential airplane. The chief White House usher. The night telephone operator in charge of information at the Department of Agriculture. The receptionist to the co-ordinator of blueprints of the American Battle Monuments Commission. . . .

✳ *The Bureaucrat's Duties*

WHAT DO all these people do in their working hours?
They *implement*.

Implementing is whatever anyone on the federal pay-roll is doing when he is handling paper, which is most of the time. If the President orders troops to Lebanon, the Pentagon implements by preparing a great many papers, some of which instruct soldiers to go to Lebanon. If the Secretary of Agriculture orders a study of American eating habits, his clerks implement by preparing a report showing that in a seventy-year lifetime the average American consumes 6,000 loaves of bread, 4 sheep, 300 chickens, 3 oxen, 12,000 pounds of vegetables, 9,000 pounds of potatoes, 14,000 pounds of fruit, 6,000 quarts of milk, 5,000 eggs, 8,000 pounds of sugar, and 2,000 pounds of cheese. (The statistics are from a Department of Agriculture study of American eating habits.)

When two or more federal employees stop imple-menting and start talking, they are *co-ordinating*.

Co-ordinating requires a big part of the workday. Its purpose is to find out who is implementing what.

For example, after the Secretary of Agriculture has ordered his survey of eating habits, several deputies must determine which divisions of the Department will handle the work. It will be necessary to keep progress checks on the division studying cheese consumption and on the division studying potato consumption. Someone must take care lest the people studying chicken con-sumption get bogged down duplicating the work of the people studying oxen consumption. All this is called co-ordinating.

The Bureaucrat's Duties

A third consuming duty of the government worker is *formulating*.

Formulating is producing ideas to be implemented.

Usually formulating is a committee operation requiring the collective thinking capacity of thousands. Each January, for instance, the President must report to Congress on the state of the Union and suggest ways for improving it. Dozens of ideas must be formulated for his speech. This ties up a big part of the bureaucracy through the late fall and early winter.

All the ideas must, of course, be co-ordinated before they are finally formulated. Once co-ordinated, they are submitted to the President's ghost writers, who sew them together crazy-quilt fashion, co-ordinating among themselves all the while. When their speech is finally implemented, it is *circulated* to the agencies for another round of co-ordinating, then returned to the ghost writers for a final implementing of the co-ordinators' decisions—or, a rewrite. What comes out is, inevitably, an atrocious speech.

From this a fourth important duty of the bureaucrat becomes manifest. He *circulates*.

Circulating is the passing from one office to another of the millions of pieces of paper that hold the government together. An eternal tornado of paper whirls inside the government and, not surprisingly, the circulating system often breaks down. The State Department proposals for the 1959 State of the Union speech were cir-

culated toward the desk of Robert Gray at the White
House, but wound up in the circulation system of Gor-
don Gray at the O.C.D.M., whence it took days to re-
trieve them.

A fifth activity of the government worker is *referring*.

Referring is usually done on the telephone. When
someone telephones the government worker for information or help, the person receiving the call refers him
to another government office, preferably in another
agency. It is done in a self-assured, no-nonsense manner.
"I will refer you to Mr. Clark in the Bureau of Yards
and Docks," the referrer says after interrupting the caller's story, and gives him Clark's number.

Clark then refers him to a party in the Federal
Power Commission, who refers him to a man in the
Pentagon, who refers him to an extension in the Weather
Bureau, which refers him to a fellow in the White House.
At any moment during the Washington workday, the
telephone wires are laden with desperate men being referred from bureaucrat to bureaucrat. Usually the chain
breaks when one party is "tied up in conference" and
his secretary promises that he will call back. If he does
call back, he will then refer the citizen to another office.
Sometimes the caller travels full circle and finds himself
referred back to Clark.

If the citizen appears in person he may be easily referred into physical collapse, for he can be sent from

one side of the building to the other and several times across Washington until spirit and strength are broken.

There are several reasons for referring. The main reason is the bureaucrat's congenital uncertainty about the extent of his own authority. A delicate problem gives him the jellied quivers, for his boss in the next echelon up may be annoyed if he says the wrong thing or angered if burdened with the caller's problem. The boss, of course, has a boss above him, who has a boss above him, with a boss above him, and each confronts the crisis of decision with agony. Their business is not deciding, but implementing, co-ordinating, formulating, and circulating.

They solve the problem by referring, or passing the crisis to someone else in an endless variation on the game of old maid.

✳ *Washingtonese: The Art of Obfuscating*

ANOTHER major occupation of the government worker is *obfuscating.*

Skill at obfuscating is essential for the man who would rise in government service, and, indeed, for almost everyone in government or out who hopes to survive long in Washington.

The object is to say nothing with euphonious flourish.

The master Obfuscator is a man who can hold an audience of important men spellbound for half an hour and send them away murmuring about his dynamism and brilliance, though he has told them nothing and though they will later quarrel among themselves about what he meant.

The mark of the great Obfuscator is an audience debating what he *meant*. The plain talker says what he means; the Obfuscator leaves them guessing.

The knack of obfuscating lies in blending ambiguous or abstruse long words in such profusion that the brain cannot retain a concrete phrase. In its highest form it has the lulling effect of water lapping gently on a lake shore. It is quite easy to master.

The basis of Obfuscation, remember, is rhythm. The rhythm must be quiet, monotonous, hypnotic, and comforting—in short, a lullaby of speech. The basic syllable with which the effect is achieved is the suffix "tion," sounding as in "nation."

When added to the end of several dozen long, vague words, all rolled into a single paragraph, the sound creates an overpowering drowsiness of the wits, just the state the Obfuscator wants to induce in his listener.

Consider a few favorite government words introduced earlier:

Implement.

Co-ordinate.

Formulate.

Actually, these words have no precise meaning. If you ask a man what has happened to that plan to send a rocket to Saturn and he tells you that it is being implemented, you still do not know what is happening to it. It may mean that the blueprints got lost in the Pentagon and are being hunted; it may mean that the rocket passed Mars at eight o'clock this morning. It may mean anything and, therefore, it means nothing. It is an exquisite instrument for obfuscating. "Co-ordinating" and "formulating" are equally superb.

Now, add the euphonious "tion" to each and you are already speaking the soothingly humming tongue of the government man. Try saying them aloud slowly: "Implementation. Formulation. Co-ordination."

Keeping these three words in mind, consider two of the more commonly used nouns: "function" and "policy." Again, these are pleasantly abstract words that set the mind roaming in search of concrete meaning. Now, putting all together, we produce a typical piece of Obfuscation:

"Policy is a function of formulation, co-ordination, and implementation."

A masterful sentence that might do credit to a presidential address. No two men could possibly agree on what it means, for it means nothing. But how wise it sounds. How learned. How soothing. Note that not a single word in the sentence produces any picture in the mind. It is pure sound.

The second characteristic of Obfuscation is *extension.*

Extension is a stretching out of short words into long words or even phrases.

The journeyman Obfuscator would never, for example, say "use." He invariably says "utilize." Or in the noun form, "utilization."

Nor does he ever say "do." In the government, you never "do." You always "effectuate."

"Make" is also bad form. The correct word is "fabricate." "Much" is always "substantial," and "later" is always "subsequently."

The rule is this: Never use a one-syllable word when a four-syllable word can be improvised. Extend! If a phrase of four or five four-syllable words comes to tongue, let it flow forth without restraint.

One important reason for extension is that short words are rarely amenable to the basic "tion" ending required to speak lullingly.

For instance, "use" cannot be extended to "usetion," but "utilize" opens out melodically into "utilization." "Make" connot be stretched into "maketion," but "fabricate" blooms naturally into "fabrication." "Do" balks at becoming "dotion," but "effectuate" glides so gracefully into "effectuation" that the tongue can scarcely be restrained.

A third characteristic of Obfuscation is the nonword. The ability to toss off non-words with aplomb is one of the graces of the true bureaucrat. Occasionally the government man finds himself in a verbal cul-de-sac where he will be forced to resort to a word that is direct, forceful, and meaningful. Rather than surrender, he will manufacture a word. The new word, sprung on the unsuspecting listener, will generally fluster him with the suspicion that his own vocabulary is threadbare, and he will probably hesitate to press for an explanation for fear of seeming ill educated.

Favorite non-words in everyday Washington use normally end in "ize." "Maximize" and "minimize" are two hackneyed examples. (What is curious about these two is their violation of the basic rule of extension. Each has only three syllables. By adding "ize" to the parent words, Obfuscators could have gained an additional syllable and created two glorious earfuls—"maximumize" and "minimumize.")

Secretary of Defense Wilson demonstrated the value of the non-word during a 1955 hearing when a congressional committee was needling him about delay in producing a certain war engine. What had happened, they wanted to know, to last year's plans for getting the thing into production? The year before, Wilson had given them the non-word treatment by telling them that the project had been "finalized." If it had been "finalized," one needler wanted to know, why wasn't the hardware ready?

"Well," replied Wilson, "that's been finalized all

right, but it hasn't been definitized yet." The committee fell back in stunned disarray, and Wilson changed the subject before they could recover.

Thousands of non-words may be manufactured on the spur of the moment by adding "ize" to a real word. It can then be extended into a longer non-word by adding the "tion" sound to the "ize."

Thus, Wilson's "definitize" becomes "definitization." His "finalize" becomes "finalization." Roll these words down the palate a few times to feel their fraudulence, noting at the same time the impossibility of imagining anyone in the act of "finalizing" or committing "definitization."

Try manufacturing a few non-words. Start with a word like "substantial," an extension of "much."

Adding the "ize," one gets "substantialize," a word that might be dropped into a speech about, say, the need for more money for prison construction. "This Administration plans to substantialize the federal prison system" would make a nice sentence.

Now add the "tion" ending and you have created "substantialization." If the money for "substantializing" the prison system has been voted and blueprints are on order, one might say: "The substantialization of the prison system is already being definitized."

No one should ever try to deal with the government in its own language!

Instead, demand that the government worker address

you in English. He will probably be rusty in English. Do not hesitate to ask him to repeat himself. Be firm.

Better yet, hire a lawyer or a lobbyist who has mastered the language, made a career of interpreting bureaucrats, and knows how to find the one in ten thousand who can solve your problem. In view of the government's passion for Obfuscation, it is not surprising that Washington has more lawyers than Philadelphia. In fact, with nearly 12,000 resident, it has as many as the entire state of Pennsylvania.

A very small percentage of these lawyers are practicing before the Supreme Court. A large proportion are hired by the government itself to help it understand what it is talking about.

✳ *The President's Peril*

THE COMMON American error is to imagine the bureaucracy as a monolithic conspiracy against enterprise and taxpayer. The error is fundamental. The American bureaucracy cannot be understood in terms of a monolith. It is rather like several hundred lidless baskets of snakes placed in a single room. There is the confusion within each basket and there is the confusion between baskets. It is anything but a master conspiracy against the world outside the room.

Intrigue and counterplot, jealousy, viciousness, profligacy—all have been known inside the government. But the meanness is rarely directed at the taxpayer—he lives in a remote world where a hundred dollars is regarded as money. It is usually directed toward a rival agency, a fellow bureaucrat, or the President.

Each agency is a distinct personality with personal aspirations, sometimes dictated by emotion, sometimes by tradition, sometimes by political pressure. The fulfillment of these aspirations inevitably requires money. Getting that money becomes a continuing obsession.

There are two ways of getting the money. The happier is to convince the President of the need and persuade him to ask Congress for the full amount. The other is to lobby Congress when the President's back is turned. Because all the agencies are competing for a limited fund at the President's disposal, each naturally regards the others with suspicion and, occasionally, malice. The agency rejected at the White House broods over the triumphs of its luckier competitors and schemes to have its own allowance raised by Congress.

To stop this sort of thing the President puts at the top of each agency a faithful colleague, chosen for loyalty to him or because his attitude toward the domain is consistent with the President's. His task is to compel order and see that the bureaucrats toe the mark drawn by the White House.

The most troublesome assignment is the Pentagon. Because of its size, complexity, and the entrenched power of competing military services, the Secretary of Defense faces an almost hopeless task.

The Eisenhower administration haplessly began its Pentagon relations by terrifying the Army. Determined to stop the steady rise in military costs, it elected to give first priority to building an Air Force capable of disintegrating Soviet Russia. This threat, it hoped, would deter the Russians from military adventuring, thus making it unlikely that the Army and Navy would be needed, thus permitting it to cut Army and Navy spending.

The Air Force was to get the lion's share of the money, though for decency's sake it continued to insist that it needed more. The Army was subjected to a series of manpower cuts and was repeatedly denied money it claimed to need for modernization. In a well-run bureaucracy, the Army's lips would have been sealed by the Secretary of Defense. What happened was that Congress and press began thundering with reports that a penny-pinching Administration was reducing the Army to a perilous state.

Army fears were compounded when the Administration awarded the Air Force the job of developing, and of fighting with, long-range missiles, thus handing it the weapon of the future just as the airplane was becoming obsolete. When the Administration propounded a bill to promote unification of the services—long an Air Force project—the Army began to suspect that the general on

Pennsylvania Avenue had forsaken it. When the Secretary of Defense conceded that he was studying a proposal to give the Air Force control of the Navy's submarine-launched Polaris missile, the always suspicious Navy began to grumble.

The Army and Navy had a powerful protector in Congress, which could not only subject the President to abuse but could also give the two aggrieved services the money that the President refused to request for them. Their complaints could be openly recited, thanks to congressional committee processes requiring that each service's military chief appear at the Capitol to testify on his budget.

The Administration moved to silence the malcontents by reminding the officers that disagreement with White House budgeting amounted to disloyalty against the Commander in Chief. Congress did not think well of this. It reminded the White House in its ponderous way that it, the Congress of the United States, was providing salaries for military officers and that it had a right to know what kind of professional judgment it was getting in return.

The Administration compromised by advising the disgruntled brass that it would be disloyal to volunteer complaints about the budget but perfectly proper to testify according to conscience's dictates if asked in committee whether a specific budgetary item was adequate.

Under this code an officer could not open his testimony with a statement like "Senator, the President's
budget, if left as he submits it, will mean the atrophy of
the Army and the destruction of the Navy as a combat
force." But suppose a senator asked: "General, is the
$220,000 allotted for boot hobnails enough to guarantee
a well-shod fighting force?" The witness could properly
reply: "In response to your direct inquiry, sir, it is well
below the minimum required to assure an adequate national defense."

Now, suppose the Army were really alarmed about
its allotment for boot hobnails. What chance would
there be that a senator might ask the one question permitting a complaint? The brass faced the problem of
getting congressmen to ask the right questions.

The ways of the bureaucracy for manhandling its
political superiors are of oriental subtlety, and the
Army and Navy were masters of the game. Senator
Hugh Scott, in a newsletter to his constituents, described
the technique they developed:

"Washington ways are peculiar. The longest way
round is often the shortest distance between the two
points of desire and achievement.

"For example: Each branch of the military, as is
natural, feels keenly the need for more weapons and
weapons research than planned in its share of the defense
budget. But no military chief before a Congressional

committee may offer unsolicited testimony designed to get more than the budget allowances for his branch of the Service.

"By some process other than mind reading, Senators and Representatives probe for information as to whether the witness feels that more weapons are necessary to the defense function of his branch of the Army, Navy or Air Force.

"The witness heaves an invisible sigh of relief and cuts loose for more hardware, with this now familiar Washington phrase: 'In response to your *direct* inquiry, sir . . .'

"While this approach is developing into standard operating procedure, what are the lower military echelons doing?

"In the quiet watches of the post-cocktail hours, they are providing grist and data to the champions of the respective services on the Hill (i.e., Congress), including quite a few Presidential candidates. These 'Presidential availables' burgeon weekly with impressive dossiers of urgent and vital needs for one favored service or another."

It should be clear that the bureaucracy has little time for conspiring against the taxpayer. It is determined to refer him, true. But its energies are consumed in conspiring within itself to frustrate a hostile sister and earn the triumph for the special interest whose philosophy it champions.

In a sense, the agencies are all arms of the President. If there is a common design among them, it is to win his mind to their causes or to frustrate him when a hostile rival has charmed him away.

It is not the enterprising taxpayer who has the most to fear from the bureaucracy. It is the poor fellow in the White House.

6

Diplomatic Circles

THE STATE DEPARTMENT is housed in a huge new $60,000,000 boxlike structure of glass, steel, and cement in a reclaimed slum area known as Foggy Bottom. Situated between two heavily trafficked, high-speed thoroughfares—Virginia and Constitution avenues—it may easily be mistaken for a pharmaceutical factory. In fact, it is the senior department of the bureaucracy. It is probably more widely known around the earth than any other arm of the government except the presidency

and may well be more important than any but the White
House.

The State Department has four functions. These are:

1. Getting along with Congress.
2. Getting along with foreign governments.
3. Getting along with Americans.
4. Reacting.

✳ *Getting Along with Congress*

ONE OF Washington's most preciously guarded secrets is
the State Department's list of summer tours abroad ar-
ranged for itinerant congressmen. Newsmen have fer-
reted out the Department's most baleful diplomatic secrets, but their annual attempts to get the congressional
junket schedule inevitably break against an iron secrecy.
Within the Department the list is handled like nitro-
glycerine. Each man understands that its revelation may
blow himself and big pieces of United States foreign
policy to kingdom come.

Not because the list is inherently scandalous. It is
not. What is unthinkable is that the State Department
would ever peach on a congressman, especially on a congressman's plans to tour at government expense. Many
congressmen are as sensitive to the charge of "junketeering" as to night-club photographs showing them with

blondes not their wives. They would not be pleased to have it published back home that they planned a frolic in Paris or Hong Kong at the Treasury's expense. They would be particularly displeased with the State Department if it were the source of such reports. Few things are more perilous for the State Department than a displeased congressman.

The reason for this bears explaining for those who may wonder why State spends so much of its diplomatic energy on Congress when the Russians are so available. First, the State Department is unique among government agencies for its lack of public supporters. The farmers may be aroused if Congress cuts into the Agriculture Department's budget. Businessmen will rise if Congress attacks the Commerce Department. Labor restrains undue brutality toward the Labor Department; the Chamber of Commerce, assaults upon the Treasury. A kaleidoscope of pressure groups make it unpleasant for the congressman who becomes ugly toward the Department of Health, Education, and Welfare. The congressman's patriotism is always involved when he turns upon the Defense Department. Tampering with the Post Office may infuriate every voter who can write.

With all these agencies, the congressman must constantly check the political wind and trim his sails accordingly. No such political restraint subdues his blood when he gazes upon the State Department in anger.

In many sections he may even reap applause from

press and public for giving it a good lesson. After all, the money dispensed by State goes not to the farmer, the laborer, or the businessman, but to *foreigners*. Not only do these foreigners not vote for American congressmen; they are also probably ungrateful for Uncle's Sam's bounty. And are not the State Department men who dispense this largesse merely crackpots and do-gooders who have never met a payroll? Will not the righteous congressman be cheered at the polls if he reminds them to get right with America and if he saves the taxpayer some money by spoiling a few of their schemes? The chances are excellent that he will.

The result is that the State Department's perpetual position before Congress is the resigned pose of the whipping boy who expects to be kicked whenever the master has had a dyspeptic outing with his wife. People in this position do not offend the master by relating his peccadilloes to the newspapers. State keeps the junketeering list a secret.

The Department expects and receives no thanks from Congress for its discretion. Congress is a harsh master. State is expected to arrange the touring Cicero's foreign itinerary; its embassies are expected to supply him with reams of local money to pay his way; embassy workers are expected to entertain him according to his whim, frequently with their savings for the children's college tuition.

But come the next session of Congress, State can expect only that its summer guest will bite its hand when it goes to the Capitol asking money for diplomatic entertaining expenses abroad or for living expenses for its diplomats. The congressman who, in Paris, may have stuffed his wallet with enough franc notes to paper the roof of Notre-Dame will systematically scream that a $200 increase in entertainment allowance for a second secretary is tantamount to debauchery of the Treasury.

In the matter of money State's most unrelenting watchdog during the Eisenhower years was Representative John J. Rooney, of Brooklyn, who controlled the purse for diplomatic administrative expenses. Diplomats stayed up nights thinking of ways to attain peaceful coexistence, not with Nikita Khrushchev, but with John Rooney. Nothing worked. In the most confidential whispers ambassadors told of techniques they had tried to bring Rooney around—friendly persuasion, groveling abasement, pressure subtly exerted through other powerful congressmen, tales of heartbreak and penury among a threadbare diplomatic corps. Rooney remained untouched.

"The trouble," explained Loy Henderson, then Deputy Undersecretary for Administration, "is that when we get into an argument with him about this thing, it always turns out that Rooney knows more about our budget than we do."

One year the Department collected a file of case histories to document its argument that men in the field were paying the government's entertainment bills out of personal income. News of the project reached the press. Next day, reports went through the Department that Rooney had been outraged by what he considered a patent attempt to put public pressure on him for increased entertainment allowances and had sworn an oath that, that year, expense allowances would not rise a dollar. They didn't.

The Department's constant fight with the House for money is a polite minuet compared with its periodic bloody engagements with the Senate. Armed with constitutional power to negate the Executive's foreign policy, the Senate carries a big stick and is easily provoked to use it on the State Department's back, or on the head of the Secretary of State.

With its power to investigate, the Senate can paralyze the Secretary by keeping him in a state of perpetual testimony before committees, as it did with Dean Acheson. John Foster Dulles escaped by keeping his personal show on the road and because Lyndon Johnson, who was then operating the Senate, refused to let it become an Inquisition. During Dulles's first two years in office, while Republicans ran the Senate, the Department was at the mercy of men who had thirsted for its blood since 1945.

An internal police operation managed by Scott McLeod, a former F.B.I. man installed as security officer upon congressional insistence, was part of the vengeance.

So was the attack upon Charles E. Bohlen when Eisenhower appointed him Ambassador to Moscow. The principal mauler, however, was Senator Joseph McCarthy. Where Acheson had fought a gallant losing battle for the Department, Dulles fed the crocodile with his subordinates. Fretting privately but eschewing public defense of his terrorized bureaucrats, Dulles remained serene and detached while the hatchet men had their way.

In view of Eisenhower's reluctance to concede that anything was amiss in the Terror, it is doubtful that heroic intervention by Dulles could have produced anything but disaster for him and the country's foreign policy. In any event, the example of Acheson's trampling by the Senate did not encourage Dulles to provoke it. He elected to "get along."

During this dark chapter in State Department history, men who had offered foreign-policy ideas later proven wrong by events filled the tumbrels sent up to Capitol Hill. Their old errors of judgment were equated, in the curious logic of the time, with present treasonous intent. Their successors, absorbing the lesson, made it a point to have few ideas.

This, in turn, brought a new fashion in senatorial criticism as the Democrats took control. In the new style, the Department was berated as intellectually barren and unable to produce the vital ideas needed to outwit the Russians. For three or four years in the mid-

1950's, this complaint was heard rumbling up from the Senate floor whenever there was a dull legislative afternoon. It became smart to say that the fault was with Dulles because he would not countenance thinking done by anyone but himself.

An equally tenable thesis is that the dearth of new thought was created by the Senate's own penchant for crucifying anyone whose ideas seem unorthodox to the next generation.

✳ *Getting Along with Foreigners*

THERE ARE ninety-eight foreign embassies and legations in Washington. They range from the Soviet Embassy on Sixteenth Street, a gray shuttered pile suggesting a funeral-accessories display house, to what Congressman Rooney has called "that monstrosity on Thirty-fourth Street," the modern cement-and-glass chancery of the Belgians.

Here is the world of the chauffeured limousine and the gossip reporter, of caviar on stale crackers and the warm martini, of the poseur, the spy, the party crasher, and the patriot, of the rented tails, the double cross, and the tired Lothario.

Into its chanceries each day pour reports from ministries around the earth and an endless stream of home-office instructions on how to handle Uncle Sam in an infinite variety of contingencies. Here are hatched plans for getting a share of the American bounty, the secret of the anti-missile missile, or an invitation to dinner. Out of it each week go hundreds of thousands of words purporting to inform home ministries about what is really happening inside Washington. Some, like the British and the French, maintain an elaborate system of personal contacts and have experts constantly studying special areas of the American scene. Other embassies cable home *The New York Times* without changing a comma.

Each has its peculiar style. The Soviet Embassy is popularly regarded as Russian espionage headquarters. When Ambassador Mikhail Menshikov took it over in 1957 from Georgi Zaroubin, he made a determined effort to change this idea. Menshikov hit Washington with a TV announcer's grin and a hearty handclasp. To everyone's astonishment he seemed no more like the run-of-the-mine Russian ambassador than George Babbitt was like Fyodor Pavlovitch Karamazov.

Where his predecessors had glowered, Menshikov smiled. Where they had affected the bleak social style of embalmers' assistants, Menshikov went abroad gorgeous in white tie and tails. Overnight he became the most available man in Washington. Speeches by the Soviet ambassador became the vogue as he obliged rural Maryland Rotarians and National Press Club alike. In Senator Joseph McCarthy's phrase, it was the most unheard-of thing ever heard of. A newspaperman who met him at a reception swore that he asked Menshikov: "What should we call you?" And that Menshikov replied: "Just call me Mike."

"Smilin' Mike" was the sobriquet Washington gave him. His English was usable and he used it fearlessly. Toasting in champagne one night at the embassy, he hoisted his glass to a senator's wife and gaily cried: "Up your bottom!" For a few giddy months that coincided with one of Moscow's smiling moods, he was the sensation of Washington. At the State Department, hard-bitten Russian experts complained that the Capitol was out of its wits. Newspaper punditry was inspired to remind everyone that Judas, too, had been able to smile.

The Menshikov interlude ended as larks with the Russians usually end. Finding peaceful coexistence temporarily unsuitable because of domestic politics, Moscow resumed scowling and "Smilin' Mike" dropped quietly out of the press except for an occasional story reporting that he had been stoned somewhere in the Middle West.

The most inscrutable embassies are the Arabs', and the most inscrutable of the Arabs are the Saudi Arabians. When King Saud visited Washington, the overwhelming question consuming the press was the size of his family. Rumor had it that his children numbered in the hundreds. The State Department was little help on this, or on much else about Saudi Arabia. A reporter who consulted a Middle East information officer for routine vital statistics got nowhere until the State Department man produced from his bottom desk drawer a brochure published by the Arabian-American Oil Company. "This is where I get my information from," he confided. "But bring it right back. It's the only copy I've got."

The size of Saud's family was still being debated when the King appeared for his first meeting with Eisenhower. When it ended, a dusky sheik in desert robes flowed into Hagerty's office to report on the interview. The massed reporters brushed aside the customary bromides about Saudi-American friendship to bore in on the central question. How many children did the King have?

"Twenty-one," replied the sheik.

And how many of these were sons?

"Twenty-five," the sheik replied.

"Do you mean to tell us," a reporter asked, "that the King has twenty-one children, twenty-five of whom are sons?"

The sheik smiled and murmured: "That is precisely correct."

The Egyptians are noted for elusiveness of language. When Dag Hammarskjold was negotiating the Middle East peace after Israel's 1956 invasion of Egypt, he soon found himself speaking the mysterious phrases of Cairo, a language as anarchic as Casey Stengel's. The reports of President Nasser's pledges which Hammarskjold was relaying from Cairo to Washington became increasingly incomprehensible to other diplomats, including the Israeli Foreign Minister, Mrs. Golda Meir. Finally he reported that Nasser was ready to make a concrete commitment in return for Israeli concessions. "All right," Mrs. Meir told Dulles, "but tell Nasser we want it in good plain Egyptian and not in Hammarskjold English."

After brief exposure to the embassy reception line, one senses that America's relationship with the world community is roughly like that between the rich man and his poor kin. Behind his back they may gossip about him as a *nouveau riche* wanting style and breeding. At the same time they are jostling constantly for special position in his esteem.

Thus, the British work to maintain the special status of senior partner, while thirteen other Atlantic Treaty nations try to keep the British from acquiring special status. If the British make the atomic bomb, the French must also make it, for it is the membership key to Uncle Sam's most exclusive club. If the Secretary of State has urgent business in London, he must make trips of equal duration to Paris and Bonn or the French and Germans will become suspicious.

The Russian dreams of sitting down alone with Sam and deciding the future of all the rest of the family, which is just a bunch of damned small-bore nuisances anyhow.

The Latin Americans live with the torment of Sam's neglect and some despise him for it. As the poor but loyal sharers of his hemisphere, they claim a special right to his good will. He treats them, instead, in the traditionally absent-minded manner of the tycoon toward poor cousins.

The Chinese Nationalists, despite having frittered away a continent, have been forgiven and blessed. Still they live in constant fear that jealous cousins may persuade Sam to throw them into the street. The Secretary of State must be at pains to tell them frequently that they are still beloved. The Chinese Communists are unregenerate black sheep, lobbing bricks through the windows, writing bad checks, and dropping banana peels in Sam's path. Given the chance, they would probably not hesitate to brain him.

The young neutral nations, following the lead of India and Indonesia, suggest evangelical cousins who want Uncle to renounce materialism, get down on his knees, and pray. They are easily offended by his argument that you cannot run a world on your knees praying.

The analogy collapses, of course, if pressed too far. Families can produce some unpleasant relationships, but they are unlikely to be downright monstrous, as relationships frequently are in the global family.

Thus, the State Department is not precisely an arbiter in an extended family quarrel, but rather an institution dedicated to preventing the principals from dis-integrating each other in a moment of hysteria and converting the planet to charred and barren rock.

In Foggy Bottom this often seems just as important as keeping congressmen happy.

* *Getting Along with Americans*

EVENTUALLY many people who settle in Washington develop a taste for helping the State Department handle its business. These are in contrast to Americans who do not settle in Washington and know the State Department only through the headlines. These usually want it dismantled, investigated, or outlawed, and the job of dealing with them is essentially the job of getting along with Congress.

The helpful type can often be just as troublesome as the hostile. The course of their rise to nuisance usually begins with acquisition of a conversational knowledge of foreign affairs. Invitations follow, leading into the homes of State Department workers and into the embassies. Soon they are traveling in what the press calls "diplomatic circles."

After moving awhile in "diplomatic circles," certain easily predictable things will happen:

1. Kiwanis in suburban Maryland will invite you to address them. They will suggest that you speak on any of the following topics:

a) "Wanted—A New Foreign Policy for the United States."

b) "How the Democrats sold out 600,000,000 Chinese."

c) "The Case for Impeaching the Secretary of State."

d) "The British Conspiracy against Uncle Sam."

e) "Stalin was Really Murdered."

f) "Let's Show the Flag in Red China."

You will ignore their list and develop your own lecture. It will be called "Geological Factors in the Development of Middle East Nationalism" or "Consular Activities in Nineteenth-Century Africa."

2. Agents of assorted rebellions around the world will begin appearing at your elbow. They will demand to know what you, as an American, are doing to force your government to overthrow their government and install them in its place. You will learn to cultivate a despairing shrug, which simultaneously suggests great sympathy (some of these gentlemen have ugly police records and quick tempers) and disgust for the blockheadedness of the current Secretary of State.

3. The French will have you to lunch at the embassy. It will be superb.

4. The British will size you up carefully, after which they will probably not have you to lunch.

5. The Russians will invite you out to lunch, but only at fixed intervals. The intervals will be fixed in

Moscow. When peaceful coexistence is on for a few months, you will be notified by an invitation from someone in the Soviet Embassy to come to lunch. It will be at the most expensive restaurant the host knows. At first you will go with flutters of anticipation. These will quickly pass. Going to lunch with a Russian is entirely an occasion of the stomach. He means to eat, and not rehash of the cold war. He may punctuate his fork work with talk about literature, his children, or his last diplomatic assignment. On politics and everything else that interests you about Russia, he will recite verbatim whole editions of *Pravda*.

6. You and your wife will start receiving invitations to attend embassy receptions. This will seem flattering. The host ambassador sees it differently. The people he wants to meet are invited to small occasions. The reception is his catchall for the hundreds whom he feels he should have in for a weak drink and a stale canapé once a year, the flotsam of the diplomatic colony.

7. Washingtonians who move in "political circles" will begin to watch you with amused contempt. In the Washington social order, those who move in "diplomatic circles" are considered longhairs and those in "political circles" men with hair on their chest (non-crackpots, do-badders, men who have met a payroll, etc.). The politically oriented hold the classic attitude of the hairy-chested toward longhairs. Hence, you are likely to find them dismissing you as an ineffective dandy out of touch

with reality, reality being how southern Illinois feels about the big butter-and-egg bill. You, in turn, will begin to find the political set exceedingly petty. The pressures the fellaheen are putting on the current Middle East dictator will seem immensely important, while the pressures the Middle West is putting on Congress to cut the foreign-aid bill will seem distressingly vicious politics.

8. You will become either pathologically violent about or indecently devoted to the Secretary of State. If the former, you will denounce the Senate as criminally complacent for not halting the legislative process and crucifying the Secretary. If enamored, you will see behind every word mildly critical of your man's any act a plot to malign a noble soul. In either case, you will become a crank or a common scold.

9. You will become learned about one small area of international affairs and become unbearable when elucidating the folly of current American policy in your pet field. Eventually you will try to correct the Secretary's misconceptions. The foreign-affairs field with its concomitant areas of propaganda and international economics is wide enough to offer everyone some small patch of ground about which he may presume to give the Secretary expert advice. It is a pastime anyone may enjoy.

If you are vocal enough about it, you will probably be asked someday to testify before the Senate Foreign Relations Committee or to join a special government commission writing a report. Your report will be referred to the State Department's Policy Planning Staff, classified "Secret," and filed for future reference, circa 1984.

This will probably pique you and tempt you to "leak" tidbits to the papers. They will give it full play. ("Leaked" documents, regardless of triviality, are heady brew to the press.) You will be investigated by the security police, and the Secretary will be asked a question about you at his news conference. Thus the evolution from neophyte to expert in the Washington world of foreign affairs. Thus, usually, his disposal by the State Department.

* *Reacting*

BESIDES fencing with the Russians and Congress and fending off lay experts, the State Department has a fourth major function.

It must "react."

"Reacting" is primarily a service for the American press, which looks upon the State Department as a vast brain receiving instantaneous impulses from a global nervous system and responding with exclamations of "Ouch!" or "Goodie!" or "Oh, oh!" according to the sensation leaping through its ganglia.

Let the Sultan of Oman announce that his legions

intend to march on the Imam of Yemen and teletype orders clack into Washington news bureaus to get "reaction" from the State Department. Nikita drops into the Persian Embassy in Moscow for a drink, confides he has just got off a letter to Washington, and ten thousand editors instantly want to know what the State Department makes of it.

Obviously, the State Department makes nothing of it. Probably Nikita's plans are divulged to it for the first time by the reporter demanding "reaction." The logical reply would be: "Since we have not received this letter yet, it is impossible to tell you what it means. Please call back next week."

Logic, however, is not an important aspect of Washington life. Moreover, the State Department fears the "propaganda triumph" that Nikita would supposedly win if his letter were allowed to occupy the headlines without rebuttal for five days. The Department feels compelled to compete for space on Page One, and so it "reacts."

Usually it has blessed little information to "react" to. Yet, even knowing nothing at all, it can exploit the editor's demand for copy to its own advantage without uttering a word that it can be held to. To demonstrate how, let us resort briefly to fantasy, though a fantasy in which many State Department reporters will recognize truth.

Reacting

During the Eisenhower administration the government developed a technique for helping the bewildered bureaucrat answer inquiries about his agency's business. It composed lists of hypothetical questions the public was likely to ask, and accompanied each with the reply that the bureaucrat should recite.

Here is how the State Department's question-and-answer sheet might have read during the 1950's for a situation in which a reporter telephoned for "reaction" to a letter from Khrushchev. It will be seen that the Department rebuffs the Russians on Page One without saying anything, or even really knowing what they are up to:

Question: I understand that a new letter from Khrushchev to the President has been delivered at the Department. Can you give me some guidance on what it says?

Answer: The letter is very long and written in Russian. It has not yet been translated.

Q: But someone must have scanned it and written a preliminary summary in English. Can you tell me whether the Russians are changing their position on (Berlin, German reunification, disarmament, Formosa, the United Nations, the Middle East, Algeria, a summit conference, Iranian oil, etc.)?

A: On a strictly confidential basis, I can tell you that there is very little new in it. I call your attention to the speculative column written yesterday by (insert name of any pundit who wrote yesterday that the outlook for U.S.-Soviet relations is bleak).

Q: Do you mean there is nothing at all new in the Khrushchev letter?

A: It is a rehash of everything that they have offered and we have rejected in the past. Don't quote me.

Q: In effect, then, the Russians seem no more willing than ever to make concessions that might lead to a settlement of this question?

A: I would not characterize their motives. I call your attention to the fact that a very wise man once said: "The two greatest mistakes any man can make are to think that he can hold his martinis and to believe that he understands the Russians."

Q: Can I attribute that to a State Department spokesman?

A: No, sir! You may say that we will give the letter serious consideration and consult with our allies.

Q: But as a matter of fact, since it is just a rehash of everything that we have considered, consulted about, and rejected in the past, it's fair to say that this one will be rejected too, I suppose.

A: I wouldn't comment on that. (If caller seems unusually dense, a chuckle is recommended at this point, tuned to suggest that he has, with his usual perspicacity, hit the nail squarely on the head.)

Q: Well, would I be off base if I wrote that this is

just another Soviet effort to create divisive propaganda that will heighten tensions between Washington and friendly European capitals?

A: You know I can't comment on that, except to call your attention to the Secretary's press-conference remarks that this correspondence from Khrushchev has no purpose beyond attempting to divide us from our allies.

Q: Just between us now, does Khrushchev make any reference to the President's proposal on (atoms for peace, aerial inspection, agonizing reappraisal, a foregathering of humanity on the grand plateau of youth, etc.)?

A: Well now, you know that implementation of the President's proposal, as delineated in London, amplified at Singapore, revised at Geneva, and definitized in the Secretary's major policy speech at Kuala Lumpur, is always subject to modification in full consultation with the NATO Council, and any Soviet proposition to the contrary effect would have to be thoroughly scrutinized by the thramasquakkle.

Q: How's that?

A: Excuse me, will you, old boy, but my other phone's ringing and I'm all alone here. Give me a call tomorrow. Better yet, call next Sunday.

✳ *Apologia*

THE MORAL of all this is that the State Department is not so sinister as Americans think it is. At worst it may be foolish, dull, and inert, but who will say that this distinguishes it from any other government agency?

One critic of its inertia recalls a speech Ambassador Llewellyn Thompson, a specialist on the Communist bloc, made to a group of Foreign Service officers some years ago. Thompson said he wished that Americans would quit talking about the "cold war" and begin thinking of Soviet-American relations as the "hundred years' war."

"When he said that," the critical gentleman reports, "you could just see those bastards settling back in their chairs and thinking: 'Now we can put everything off for the next ninety-nine years.'"

In foolishness, State has explored the far frontiers of absurdity. A few years ago, struck by an impulse to muzzle its intelligence division in order to prevent the escape of secret information, it promulgated an edict cautioning intelligence men against communication with newspapermen.

Suppose, the directive hypothesized, that a reporter called and asked: "What is the capital of Paraguay?" Should the intelligence man forthrightly reply: "Asunción"?

No! For, the edict warned, the most innocent question could be used by a clever reporter to lead the intelligence man into betraying vital information.

This document, with its suggestion that State regarded its intelligence men as so many cretins, was deactivated amid much blushing after its exposure, but it remains a sample of what any bureaucracy is capable of.

Being the most personal and the most human of all the government's agencies, State has human strengths and virtues to match its foibles. It has its achievements too. It is pointless to enumerate these here. The Department and the White House, no matter what the Administration, will always publicize them amply.

Its greatest achievement of all is so overwhelmingly simple that it is often overlooked by an overly captious public as well as by the government's professional hucksters. The American might find it worth remembering when he is cursing the men of Foggy Bottom.

It is this: After sixteen years of the nuclear age, we are all still here.

7

The Hill

T HE AMERICAN parliament is called the Congress. It consists of 535 members who are housed in six enormous buildings on Capitol Hill, always referred to in Washington simply as the Hill. The Capitol itself is a sprawling three-story marble-and-limestone structure surmounted by a cast-iron dome and honeycombed with miles of corridors and subterranean passageways.

Here may be found two miniature subway systems, television and broadcasting studios, the world's most magnificent library, the world's most execrable art, hideaways for the country's more notorious politicians, sundry restaurants (all bad), and, over the year, the best entertainment to be had in Washington.

At last accounting, grounds, buildings, and contents of the property were valued at $2,716,714,015.62. The most valuable single item was the collection of the Library of Congress, which was assessed at $2,233,695,-000.

The Congress is extraordinary among parliaments for its peculiar relationship with the head of government. In most states, the head of government participates in his parliament, answers to it directly, and loses his office if it repudiates his policies.

In the American system, relations between President and Congress are more like affairs between hostile states. The President rarely sets foot in the place. When he does, it is only to read a speech and receive perfunctory applause.

He may dispatch notes and ambassadors urging Congress to do this or that, but Congress often ignores his suggestions and does something quite different. In such cases the President may declare its work null and void, with the result that nothing is done. Feelings often become bitter.

Congress has power to nullify the President's treaties, to reject his chosen advisers, and to deny the money that he requests to run the government. It is a quaint relationship, which requires the President to maintain one of the busiest lobbying operations at the Capitol and, often, to play the horse trader to realize his goals.

Congress is divided into two main branches, the Senate and the House of Representatives. Each house is subdivided into committees, which are ruled, frequently with an iron fist, by old men called chairmen. Chairmen can often singlehandedly kill any bill that displeases them. Obviously, it is very nice to be a chairman.

To become a chairman a man needs only to have been in office longer than anyone else who wants the chairmanship. This is known as the rule of seniority. It creates some strange situations, such as the South's death grip on most legislation whenever the Democratic party is in power.

Each house has its own set of "rules." The Senate's provide, in effect, that the Senate may not perform the duties assigned to it by the Constitution. Accordingly, whenever the Senate decides to transact some business, it normally begins by suspending the "rules."

The House's "rules" are more elaborate and often seem to have been devised by astrologists. It is not unusual to see the House so confused about its own "parliamentary situation" that even the parliamentarian has to go to the library to learn what it can do next. Often what it can do at any given moment seems to depend upon the phase of the moon.

On certain Wednesdays, for example, it may act upon bills despite the objection of the Rules Committee, but only if it can pass them before the clock strikes midnight. When the House leaders want to transact business, they select a pliable presiding officer who can be relied upon to interpret the "rules" to suit the leadership.

The duties of Congress are as follows:

1. To make the laws.
2. To approve the President's appointments.
3. To ratify treaties.
4. To levy taxes and raise revenues.
5. To investigate whatever strikes its fancy.

Sometimes Congress conducts itself on the assumption that its duties are also:

1. To extort boons from the President.
2. To bilk the Treasury.
3. To terrorize the bureaucracy.
4. To persecute anyone disliked by any influential congressman.
5. To abolish the Supreme Court.

Congressmen are immune from arrest while at or on their way to work, but are subject to capture and forcible escort to the Capitol when their presence is required on the floor. They are immune from prosecution for libel and slander committed on the floor or in committee hearings.

Lengthy service develops an imperial strain in many members. One Capitol habitué tells of meeting the aged and infirm Senator Kenneth D. McKellar in a corridor one morning and murmuring politely: "How are you today, Senator?" In reply, the old man, interpreting the words as a reflection on his failing health, raised his cane, thwacked it angrily across the fellow's collarbone, and passed on without a word.

Altogether, it is a very odd society.

✳ *Baroque-ialism*

CONGRESS is a cantankerous, old-fashioned institution apt to be looked upon in this nervous age as a museum piece. Its manner is as elaborately courteous as a Savannah lawyer's. After his first few weeks in the Senate, Edmund S. Muskie told a Boston audience what he had learned about the etiquette of proper address during debate.

If you and another senator are in perfect agreement, he explained, "you address him merely as 'the senator from such-and-such a state.' If you are not too sure he agrees wholly with you, you should refer to him as 'the able senator from ——.' But if you know there is violent disagreement on an issue, there is only one way to address him: 'the able and distinguished senator, my friend from ——.' "

The Senate's rhetorical style derives from the mighty thunder of the nineteenth-century stump orators. The prim understatement of the twentieth century is rarely admitted. Overstatement trimmed with gingerbread is the accepted form, and metaphorical orgy is commonplace.

"The question is, Who stole the wheelbarrow?" Senator Everett Dirksen, a Republican, roared at the peak of a typical debate on government spending. The scoundrel, he went on, was the Democratic party. "No red herring, no matter how upholstered or embroidered it may be, is going to wash out that contention," he declared.

Senator Warren Magnuson, soaring to peaks of rhetoric in another debate, came to this thundering climax: "It is time to take the bull by the tail and look the situation squarely in the face!"

Congress's humor is the broad, back-country brand of the last century and is very likely to fall ponderously on the modern ear. It is Senator Tom Connally summarizing his objections to Generalissimo Chiang Kai-shek in these words: "The trouble with ole Chiang is: not enough general-ing and too much issimo-ing."

And it is Senator Dirksen retelling the story of the caller who visited Huey Long one afternoon at his hotel to find the Kingfish fretting about humanity's ingratitude. From the time of Christ, Long declared, men had abused their saviors, crucifying Jesus, and burning, beheading, and hanging others. "Sometimes," said the Kingfish, glaring at his caller, "it just seems like man don't *want* to be saved from himself, but goddam him, I'm gonna save him anyhow!"

Senator Robert Kerr, describing a quiet witness whose testimony was a single sentence of agreement with three hours of contradictory filibustering by his boss, compared him to a boy who had been asked about his father's dying words. "He didn't have any," the boy replied. "Maw was with him to the end."

When Secretary of Defense McElroy suggested a law to prevent the military services from expressing disagreement with the defense budget, Senator Sam Ervin was reminded of the justice of the peace hearing a civil suit. "After hearing the plaintiff," Ervin said, "the justice of the peace turned to the defendant and said: 'I'd appreciate it very much if you would not present your case. When I hear both sides it gets me confused and I have trouble making up my mind.'"

Lyndon Johnson, complaining that Republicans were on both sides of a budget argument, told the Senate they reminded him of an unemployed Texas schoolteacher who applied to a hill-country school board. "We would like to retain your services," they told him, "but tell us this: There is some difference of opinion in our community about geography, and we want to know which side you are on. Do you teach that the world is round, or do you teach that the world is flat?" And the applicant, Johnson went on, immediately replied: "I teach it either way."

Here is Senator Hugh Scott, commenting on Senate

debate: "A man gets up to speak and says nothing. Nobody listens. Then everybody disagrees."

Corn abounds. For years Senator Kerr mailed his constituents each week a homespun aphorism suitable for framing in embroidery over horsehair sofas. "To strive for justice is to succeed, even if you fail" was a typical "Kerr Kernel." And, "Unless we believe in something, we are nothing. The more we believe in, the more we become." And, "There is a vast difference between sitting up and taking notice, and just sitting."

When Senator Alexander Wiley received an abusive letter from a constituent, he responded in verse, then proudly read his work on the Senate floor.

> *"It is good that folks like you and me,*
> *Can agreeably disagree,*
> *Over our political and religious thought.*
> *A few years back we would have fought,*
> *And blood would have been shed.*
> *Now we have law instead,*
> *And arbitrary power is checked,*
> *So liberty will not be wrecked.*
> *The Constitution stands supreme,*
> *Let those who will, snort and scream."*

When Representative Coya Knutson of Minnesota wanted to invite Speaker Sam Rayburn of Texas to vacation in her state, she borrowed *Hiawatha*'s meter

147

and had her invitation published in the *Congressional Record*. A sample verse:

"Minn-e-so-ta wants you, needs you. Say the word and come to see us.

The fulfillment is greater than whatever I can promise.

Let us share the peace primeval. Let us drop the cares that vex us.

We would sure be glad to have you—Mr. Speaker, Sam of Texas."

Appropriately, Congress is housed in Washington's most baroque quarters. The design and furnishings might have been personally selected by a tycoon of the Gilded Age. Its dome, a worthy imitation of Wren, is surmounted by a piece of statuary apparently modeled from a cigar-store Indian. The closest inspection is required to see that it is not a cigar-store Indian at all, but a symbolic female figure, draped in what looks to be a fringed tablecloth, representing Freedom. The interior fittings are in the same spirit.

The Capitol's central corridor, extending more than seven hundred feet between House and Senate chambers, is packed with an assortment of statuary that would have looked fitting thirty-five years ago on a bootlegger's lawn. Here is a bust of Aysh-Ke-Bah-Ke-Ko-Zhay, a Chippewa Indian. Here, another of Harry Truman, unrecognizable without his eyeglasses. Here is Huey Long, frozen in all his tousled glory in mid-speech. Further along stands a frontiersman, twice life size, his fringed buckskins taut against straining muscles as he lunges fiercely at passing congressmen. And here the despotic Pat McCarran, adorned in a bronze smile of sweet saintliness and the robes of justice.

The offices, conceived in Victorian grandeur, are filled with bulging oak desks, marble fireplaces overhung with enormous mirrors, great sparkling glass chandeliers, and the faint aroma of fine cigars.

The House chamber is the building's most conspicuous effort to escape the nineteenth century, and the result is uninspiring. A barnlike room decorated in light blue and chocolate, it lacks charm and character. The smaller Senate chamber is a more intimate place of snuffboxes, spittoons, desks reminiscent of the early American schoolroom, and deep leather sofas tucked in the corners.

In the Senate anything may happen at any moment. In the middle of the tensest debate, the senior senator from Nevada may render an ode to a retired prospector. Not so long ago, one knight of the old West strode through the cloakroom's swinging doors and collapsed face first on the Senate floor in an alcoholically induced motor-reflex failure. Twenty bills may be passed, with the casual visitor in the gallery none the wiser, while there are only three or four members on the floor.

Most bills, in fact, pass the Senate in this unobtrusive fashion. Two senators from each party comb the mountain of pending legislation and cull out the bills about which there is no controversy. All members are privately notified that these bills will be placed on the "calendar" and passed at a specified time unless there is objection. If objection is made, the bill is held back for debate, or until its sponsor can quietly win over the objector.

At the appointed time, the Senate Majority Leader reads off the "calendar" number of each cleared bill and with a tobacco auctioneer's mumble asks that it be considered as having been read a third time and passed without objection. In this way, it is possible to pass a hundred bills in half an hour with only a few hands on the floor.

In general, the Capitol still lives by such labyrinthine procedures conceived nearly two centuries ago and not much changed today. Its actions are planned and executed in an environment suffused with the past. Congress is commonly imagined as a non-stop brawl pitting an occasional hero against packs of dastards, but most often clown against clown. It is subtler than that. After long exposure, many Washingtonians conclude that it is a calm, old-fashioned place where dignity and insistence on doing things with proper form contribute a serene, reflective quality to the American process, and that this may even be worth preserving.

✻ *The Persecuting Minority*

IT WILL HELP understanding of the Congress to discard the notion that the Capitol is the temple of majority rule.

The Founders were candid about their distaste for majority rule and purposely designed the Senate as a bulwark to protect the minority against excesses of the mob. Statistics illustrate the point in the 1960's. About half the American population, roughly 90,000,000 persons, is contained in ten states. In the Senate, these 90,000,000 are represented by twenty votes, only one fifth of the membership.

The ten least populous states, with a combined population of only about 5,00,000, also have twenty votes. Theoretically, this scattered minority, smaller than the population of Los Angeles, could cancel the power of half the population.

Because the heavily populated states usually have the kind of problems that bore the underpopulated, the big-state leaders tend to look upon the Senate as an archaic institution whose abolition could only promote the national welfare. The small states cherish it as the treasured repository of powers they can attain nowhere else.

In theory, the popular majority expresses its will in the House of Representatives. The reality is somewhat different, for the shrinking rural population is represented far out of proportion to its size and at the expense of the expanding urban centers. Moreover, a stratified power structure in the House lodges immense authority in the hands of a few—usually Southerners or men from small one-party states—and makes it difficult for the herd to do more than shuffle restlessly.

When the oppressed masses of the House break loose, as they sometimes do, the carnage may be impressive. In 1946, seized with one of its periodic hysterias, the House stampeded and with scarcely a coherent word of discussion passed a bill empowering the President to draft striking union members into the Army. The provocation was a railroad strike that had infuriated President Truman and angered much of the population against locomotive engineers. Under color of patriotic outrage, the majority heatedly whooped through the kind of solution that comes naturally to dictators and lynch mobs.

The Senate saved the situation. Robert A. Taft, the labor movement's fork-tailed Satan, announced in the midst of the uproar that he saw no need for hasty action. This was a bill that should be talked about, he said, and he proceeded to talk about it. While he talked, the mob spirit, as it usually does, yielded to the human urge to go home and eat, and a few days later the draft bill was unceremoniously laid aside.

Proponents of truer majority rule in Congress

usually base their case on the difficulty of getting civil rights legislation past the Senate. For years the House diligently passed comprehensive civil rights legislation and the Southern minority in the Senate just as regularly killed it.

Senators from the Northern industrial states protested that a small minority was abusing the Senate to thwart the majority will. The villain of the piece was invariably identified as the filibuster.

The filibuster today is probably the most overrated menace since the giant squid. It is the use of the Senate's tradition of unlimited debate to try to kill a bill on the floor. A determined minority may paralyze the Senate and persuade the majority to abandon its bill in return for being permitted to proceed with other business.

It is possible to cut off a filibuster if two thirds of the membership on the floor can be persuaded to vote for ending debate. The Southerners at peak strength could muster only twenty-two votes against ending debate. Assuming a full house for the vote, thirty-four votes would be required to prevent the filibusterers from being gagged. Obviously, the Southerners were getting aid and comfort from forces outside the Confederacy.

In fact, they were getting it in impressive volume. For years they had the tacit support of the Senate's economic conservatives, both Republican and Democratic. These gentleman, usually from the states without heavy Negro voting blocs to punish them, simply contracted against breaking Southern filibusters. In return, they received Southern help to defeat liberal socio-economic legislation. Since the civil rights advocates were usually also the liberals in socio-economic matters, the economic conservatives found it agreeable to make common cause with the Southerners.

It is even arguable that, despite complaints about the majority's will being frustrated on civil rights, there was actually no majority for most of the bills, that the majority of the Senate was either indifferent to the issue or sympathetic to Southern fears of punitive legislation.

The Southerners were allowed to have their way because it was easy for many non-Southern senators to escape the issue so long as they were not pinned on a roll-call vote. The civil rights battle of 1957, in which the non-Southern conservatives were finally forced to take a recorded position on civil rights, suggested that it had been connivance by non-Southerners, and not the filibuster, that had always killed rights bills in the past.

The 1957 battle was the turning point of the issue after eighty years of much talk and little action. By this time the Supreme Court's ruling against school segregation had made the race issue the most inflammable domestic issue of the 1950's. Where once it had engaged only the Negro minority and a scattering of liberals, now dangerous emotions were in play.

Southern defiance of the Court had stirred ancient memories and emotions embedded in the American char-

154

acter since 1861. Once, the issue had been a question of man's tolerance for man, an area in which parliaments had always stepped with caution and little hope. Now, the human dilemma was suffused with mighty constitutional issues involving the relative authorities of the courts, the federal government, and the states. Here were issues that had always made American blood pound and that had once involved the country in civil war, leaving wounds that were still being plucked at a hundred years later.

Against this background, it became impossible for many of the economic conservatives to contract quietly with the Southern filibusterers once more. The issue was so delicate that few politicians could refuse with impunity to be counted. And once the conservatives were flushed into the open and required to vote one way or the other, few could afford to vote for the filibuster and against civil rights, courts, and the federal authority.

The filibuster myth was exposed. If the Southerners attempted it, they would surely lose. Shrunk down to a force of only twenty-two votes, with little chance of adding more, they lacked the numbers to prevent a filibuster from being shut down by a two-thirds majority. If they attempted one, they risked spreading the emotional fires already burning in the civil rights encampment and provoking fearful vengeance upon themselves.

With defeat inevitable, they rejected the filibuster and concentrated upon making the inevitable bill as painless as possible. What finally emerged was a compromise that committed the federal government to assist the Southern Negro in reclaiming his right to vote. The filibuster as an instrument of minority intransigence had proved an overrated weapon in the first civil rights test where a majority of the Senate clearly wanted action.

One important footnote: The tradition of unlimited debate is one of the characteristics of the Senate which makes the United States senator one of the earth's unique citizens. For this reason, many senators are reluctant to tamper with it. The House of Representatives does not enjoy it, nor does the House of Commons, nor does any other parliamentary body of any distinction. In the House of Representatives, the chair may simply refuse ever to recognize a member who displeases the chairman; refusal to recognize a senator would be an unthinkably gross offense for any Vice-President.

The House normally operates under a rigid time limit. Small parcels of speaking time are allotted to a few members and they are gaveled into silence the second their time expires. A vote of the majority may terminate debate at any point. Few senators really want to have their grandeur debased to that point.

✳ *How to Be a Successful Senator*

HERE ARE a few of the more important things a new
senator must know to tide him over the first months,
when the elders will be sizing him up:

1. Use your hands. The distinguishing characteristic
of the senator is a zest for pawing and mauling all other
males within grasp, but particularly other senators. This
has been called "pressing the flesh." Upon entering the
Senate chamber, it is essential at all times to observe this
ritual of the laying on of hands. It involves shaking hands
enthusiastically with the man you have just ridden over
with on the subway, throwing an arm affectionately
around the next man to cross your path, slapping the
back of an old enemy, punching a friend jovially about
the clavicle, or seizing the biceps of the senator whose
attention you hope to command for a few moments.
When the Senate floor is crowded, the clasping and
clutching and nudging and hugging is as fierce as the action in a judo class. Senators who do not participate are
considered aloof and will probably not go far.

2. Be seen and not heard. The new man in the Senate
undergoes a trial period before the elders that may last
up to ten years. What the old-timers want to find out is
whether he is going to make a real "Senate man" or
whether he is just another upstart. Upstarts are young
men who talk too much, particularly on matters about

157

which any elder considers himself the final authority. A potential "Senate man" is one who behaves as if he might someday learn what the elders have to teach him. The elders are usually old men who are sick of listening to speeches and find them doubly annoying when delivered by whippersnappers. Whippersnappers are new senators who believe their opinions are interesting to anyone except their wives.

All senators are equal, to paraphrase Orwell, but some senators are more equal than others. The upstart must learn humility before he is permitted to share the bourbon in the club's most exclusive rooms. If he makes it, one day, while humbly nursing a glass, he will hear, as from Olympus, one of the elders ask for his opinion; at that instant, he will have finally arrived in the Senate.

3. Feel exclusive. It is the nature of the senator to be condescending in his dealings with mankind. There are gradations of condescension which should be mastered. In committee hearings, an air of celestial superiority is maintained toward all witnesses, including cabinet officers. By lowering the voice an octave and looking grave, the senator can usually induce a gratifying show of inferiority from the man in the witness chair. If the witness seems irreverent, push him around subtly. Suggest in a faintly annoyed tone that he sit up closer to the microphone. Tell him to speak louder. Have him repeat things. Frown while making pencil marks on a pad.

When dealing with the press, cultivate a mysterious

cast of eye, suggesting that you know more than you are willing to spill. Dealing with the constituent, use a hearty paternal smile. Let him feel that your wisdom about whatever interests him is so deep that it is useless to try to convey it in less than a whole day. Assure him in subtle ways that his future is in the safe hands of a good stern father.

Tell him that you and the President are discussing his problem. Presume now and then to get off a press release correcting the President or urging a new national policy. Remember, you may know that underneath the toga lurks just another lawyer married to the town embalmer's daughter, but not many other people suspect it and your colleagues will be displeased if you insist upon acting like it. All of them hide secrets equally dreadful, and it will not be appreciated if you start the governed to thinking that senators are just like people.

4. Acquire facility in a few senatorial phrases. The new man, though always urging his modesty upon the elders, must also be prepared to speak on short notice. A few dozen phrases of Senate argot will enable him to make a passable showing on his feet without really saying anything. For the first ten years it is advisable to preface the slightest observation with some self-derogatory remark like "As a junior member of this distinguished body, I hesitate to burden my able and learned colleagues . . ." From there it is relatively simple. A

few stock phrases will always produce solemn nods from all but the crankiest. The meticulous man will want to master their correct usage; however, simply by reeling off a half dozen of them with loose connectives, quite an acceptable speech can be delivered extemporaneously.

To see how, consider the following phrases:

"The power of the purse."

"Fiscal responsibility."

"Members on both sides of the aisle."

"American way of life."

"My distinguished colleague."

"In its (their) wisdom."

"All Americans will join."

"Will be responsible."

"We cannot legislate on the floor."

"Men of little faith."

See how readily these everyday Senate phrases may be adapted to any situation: Assume that you wish to speak in support of a committee recommendation to cut the Army budget. You may say: "The Constitutional Convention *in its wisdom* endowed Congress with *the power of the purse.* As *my distinguished colleague* has so ably put it, *fiscal responsibility* compels *members on both sides of the aisle* to guarantee that the Senate will ignore the *men of little faith* in the *American way of life* and not be panicked. *We cannot legislate on the floor. All Americans will join* in applauding this cut."

But suppose you want to speak against the budget

160

cut. You might say: "I must disagree with my most able, brilliant, and *distinguished colleague* who says that *we cannot legislate on the floor. In its wisdom* the Constitutional Convention bestowed upon Congress *the power of the purse. All Americans will join* in expecting that this great body *will be responsible* to its duty to safeguard *the American way of life. Members on both sides of the aisle* must agree that only *men of little faith* in the American economy could argue that *fiscal responsibility* dictates this cut."

Either makes an acceptable and perfectly uninteresting Senate speech of the sort heard any day in the Capitol's north wing. In fact, these ten phrases can carry a man through a long if unsensational career in the Senate, provided he has a ghost writer to handle his after-dinner chores.

The senator who wants to distinguish himself should become skilled in other, more specialized clichés. If he seeks a seat on the Foreign Relations Committee, he must learn to describe the Middle East as "tense," "troubled," or "explosive," and remind the State Department from time to time that it is an area "torn by ancient rivalries" or "new nationalism."

He should define the goal of foreign economic policy as "trade not aid." Now and then he must say: "Lenin wrote that the road to Paris lies through Peiping." He should urge "more flexibility" in foreign policy, remind the White House that "Africa is stirring," and scold the foreign-aid administrator for "pouring dollars down the ratholes of the world."

This does not exhaust the senatorial lexicon, but it is pointless to canvass every field. Clichés frequently enjoy a long run, then vanish abruptly from Senate speech. At the time of the first Russian sputniks, "a sense of urgency" was on every tongue. It is now passé. So is "the frontiers of science," which enjoyed tremendous vogue. For years every speech included the line "We live in a time of confusion and chaos." This has yielded to "These are dangerous times" and will probably undergo many more mutations before the Russians and Chinese are finished.

"Prophets of gloom and doom," meaning people who worry about declines in the economy, enjoyed a long life but now seems to be fading. Nevertheless, the new senator need not have an ear attuned to cliché to stay in stride with his times. Conscientious reading of the *Congressional Record* will steep his brain in clichés, and he will find after a while that he has only to open his mouth to hear them spring forth fully rounded.

✳ *The Not So Lower House*

No ONE will want to make the mistake of calling the Senate "the upper house" within earshot of a representative. Every House man holds doggedly, in the face of impressive contradictory evidence, to the constitutional thesis that Senate and House are equal. The authentic House man regards as manifestations of ignorance the journalist's insistence on lionizing the Senate and ignoring the House. He resents the easy glory that flows to the Senate's densest numskull while brilliant men of the House live and die in anonymity.

Alas for the House, the evidences of its decline lie everywhere. If one telephones a senator, the Capitol switchboard connects him immediately with the senator's office. When he telephones a representative, he is not transferred at once to the House man he seeks, but turned over to the "information" operator, just as when calling the Capitol janitor or the chief of the Senate Folding Room.

Senators are provided with two underground railways to ease their weight from the Capitol to their office suites. The House man must walk. Senators have reserved elevators in the Capitol to transport them in lonely splendor unbrushed by the herd. The House man must ride with the press. In his office building, the senator may punch the elevator button three times and get non-stop service to the floor he wants, no matter what the destinations of lesser passengers. The House man waits his turn with the stenographer.

There is other evidence. The most saddening is the vast number of representatives either pining secretly or running unashamedly for seats in the Senate. Senators never scheme to escape to the House. Indeed, let the truth be told: Senators feel superior to representatives. A plea incessantly invoked in the Senate to beat down proposals for limiting Senate debate is: "Great God! Do you want to turn the Senate into another House of Representatives?" In the Senate a man may talk until his tongue cleaves to his palate. In the House he is fortunate to be allowed five minutes on bills of the greatest importance.

The snobbishness of the Senate is not limited to its members, but extends to hangers-on. Newsmen who cover the Senate may look down upon an occasional assignment in the House as beneath their stature. William S. White, the distinguished columnist and authority on the Senate, has boasted, only half jokingly, that he has never set foot on the House's side of the Capitol.

The House suffers from two afflictions. It is too big and it has to go to the voters too often. With 435 members, it would be perpetually immobilized if granted anything comparable to the individual freedom allowed the senator. The House of Commons has more than 600 members, but it also has the gag rule to cut off debate, spartan party discipline that discourages fractionalization of voting, and the leaders of government and opposition sitting within two sword lengths of each other to focus its operations. Its members also usually have an expectation of reasonable tenure (up to five years) once they have been elected.

Because the representative must campaign for his job every two years, the House is torn and tossed by every transient public emotion. Having to go to the hustings every other autumn, the House man is never completely free of the smell of sawdust and police-station disinfectant. The constant obligation to fight for his political life gives his work the jerry-built quality of something thrown together slapdash to satisfy the demands of this afternoon's headlines. (Paradoxically, in the quiet of its committee rooms the House usually seems to do a more competent job on legislation than the Senate, where committee operations are much more loudly publicized.)

Shortly after his election to the Senate, Hugh Scott, a graduate of the House, told a university audience: "The chore of having to run for re-election every other year is so arduous that some members of Congress are relieved when they are defeated." He told of one defeated representative who was accosted by a woman on the street the day after the election. "Mr. Cole," she said, "I know you, but I bet you don't know who I am."

"No, I don't," the gentleman replied, "and I don't give a damn."

There are also certain physical distinctions between the senator and the representative. The senator is smartly tailored, pinkly barbered, and meticulously manicured. He exudes solemnity, though he be a youngster shy of thirty-five, and walks with the weighty tread of an investment banker or a bishop. He finds it impossible to listen for longer than the ghost of a moment, but he requires thousands of words circuitously strung together to discharge his own brain of the most trifling opinion.

Wherever he goes he moves with conscious dignity and hauteur. He is no mere knight, but a prince of the royal blood, charged with the mission of perpetuating the Republic against the assaults of harebrained Presidents and street mobs. In his grandest manifestations he may seem to be merely passing through on a vacation from Olympus. Senator Walter George, for example, once dismissed Herbert Brownell, to the Senate's complete satisfaction, as "a very odd little Attorney General."

The House man is another breed. Most often he has a rumpled, impecunious, off-the-rack look. He wears the harried expression of the campaigner who has fought too many battles. No senatorial solemnity for him. He lacks the time. His step is fast and his conversation brisk, for there is always another election just over the horizon and he must look to his powder and oil his blunderbuss. Compelled by the iron rules of the House to articulate his opinions on the gravest controversy within the span of five minutes, he gets to the point quickly. Intuitively, behind him he sees the Speaker's gavel prepared to cut him short when his five minutes has expired. His debates under the gun sometimes cut to the bone of a controversy with a terseness and drama rarely matched in the Senate's meandering lava of Victorian syntax.

Nevertheless, his title alone is insufficient to make the

cabinet officer quake, force managing editors to replate, or earn him the adulation of the gallery. For the most part he remains a face in the mob, temporarily displaced from city hall or courthouse and bucking for promotion to higher office—like the Senate.

On this evidence, many ignore the House under the misconception that it is the small potato of the government family. This is a mistake. Not only is the House, in its unobtrusive fashion, a worthy peer of the Senate but it also contains a nucleus of members just as powerful as the Senate's most celebrated overlords.

Ironically, these titans of the citadel of representative democracy are usually men who rarely submit to the biennial elections. Most of them represent "rotten boroughs," constituencies where two-party politics is unknown and where succession to power is, therefore, dynastic rather than elective. Under the seniority rule, power is bestowed for longevity of service. Men from two-party districts rarely achieve seniority, since a man vulnerable to challenge every two years must inevitably run afoul of the law of averages.

The small group from the rotten boroughs, running sometimes unopposed, sometimes with token opposition, stays on for twenty, thirty, and forty years, to become committee chairmen, master the mysteries of the House and make it work, or make it stall. Without them, the House might slide into chaos like the Assembly of the late Fourth French Republic.

167

These veteran lords of the House, unlike their lesser colleagues, harbor no inner suspicion that the House really is "the lower chamber." They wear a majesty of their own, which is not tarnished in their sight because the public chooses to remain ignorant of it. To them, nothing could be more contemptible than the suggestion that they might prefer to be in the Senate. In their view, the Senate is merely "the other place," and a rather disorderly one at that.

When they do business with "the other place," as occasionally they must, they go as ambassadors plenipotentiary to neutral ground and do not expect to negotiate with pipsqueaks, but with the patriarchs. These are the men whom the Senate's leaders keep in mind when they weigh the fate of an important project. The Senate floor leader may be a lord to the House's herd, but when he crosses the path of the authentic House man he treads with respect.

In the House these men are a power apart, with the might and prerogatives of feudal barons. Sometimes they are at war among themselves, sometimes they exercise tyrannical authority over the committees that are their enclaves.

Representative Carl Vinson, of Georgia, chairman of the House Armed Services Committee after more than forty-five years of service, has typified the class. He came to Congress from rural Georgia in 1914 and steadfastly resisted the polished mannerisms country boys usually acquire when they switch to low shoes, start going to cocktail parties, and begin advising Presidents. Known irreverently as "Uncle Carl," he has remained as old-fashioned as a county courthouse. His wardrobe is still upcountry "Sunday best." He has never had much patience with what passes in Washington for greatness. "Gin'rul," he has been known to say to some four-starred Horatius whose face had peered purposefully from magazine covers, "what did you say your name was?"

His power to influence the Pentagon, exercised through his committee, is immense. When someone suggested years ago that he would be the logical choice for Secretary of Defense, he replied: "Shucks, I'd rather run the Pentagon from up here." When, in public hearings, Vinson offered advice to Admiral Arleigh Burke, Chief of Naval Operations, it was received with a snappy "Aye, aye, sir." And when Secretary of Defense McElroy once undertook to tell him what should be done to reorganize the Defense Department, Vinson impatiently ended the dissertation by announcing: "You know that's not sound." McElroy did not press his point.

For years Vinson was known as the Navy's first line of defense in the internal wars that wracked the services, and like a good Navy man, he ran a taut ship in his committee room. After hearings on a controversial Pentagon reorganization bill in 1958, a committee report had to be written for submission to the House. When the committee met to approve the report, few members of the thirty-one-member group had seen it or even knew what it said. There were no copies for them to study when Vinson moved the report's adoption.

Far down the committee bench, a voice objected that it was not quite proper to ask the committee to approve something that few members had seen.

"After you have read this report," Uncle Carl replied, "you will be proud to say you had a hand in writing it."

The committee immediately voted its adoption. The vote, as usual with Vinson's committee, was unanimous.

That is the way a great House man does business.

✳ Valedictory

AFTER twenty-eight years in Congress, Senator Henry F. Ashurst got the news from Arizona that he had been defeated for re-election. Later the same day he came to the Senate floor and began to speak extemporaneously about his years in Congress and about his emotions upon his defeat. A large group of senators drifted in from the lobbies, the cloakrooms, and the corridors, took their seats, and listened, as senators rarely do. In the course of a long speech, Ashurst told them:

"Senators, you should not be disturbed by criticism of Congress. When the press, or citizens generally, criticize Congress, it is the sign of a free people. If one were a stranger to this planet, but understood somewhat human affairs, and he had made an excursion here to discover quickly and accurately what governments were free and what were despotic and autocratic, he would not look to the Treasury to ascertain what governments were free; he would not even look to the Army or the Navy. He would look to the parliament, the lawmaking body.

"If its members spoke freely, and said what they believed, and if the citizens who elected the parliament were free at all times to criticize the parliament or the Congress, these would be the signs, the symbols, and the proofs of a free people."

8

In Toga and Gumshoe

ONE OF CONGRESS's most zealously pursued duties is investigating. There are no limits on what it may investigate and very few restraints on the conduct of the congressman as investigator. He has the power of subpoena, immunity from slander and libel laws, experience in manipulating the headlines to damage his witnesses, license to ignore courtroom rules of fair play, and a corps of professional detectives financed by the United States Treasury to build his case.

The man under investigation is practically helpless.

He may have a lawyer to advise him when he testifies, but his attorney may not cross-examine hostile witnesses. He is subject to bellowing attacks, bullying, and ridicule. Many investigations amount to prosecutions, with punishment consisting of damaged reputation, public contempt, harassment, and job loss. The man being prosecuted has no right to put on a defense case or to call his own witnesses. Any testimony the congressman wants to hear is admissible, including gossip, hearsay, and the word of recognized perjurers.

In short, the rules are a prosecuting attorney's dream of Paradise, and the congressional investigation a joy to men of gauleiter mentality.

Sometimes the excesses of the pastime lead to absurdity, as in the case of Harvey Matusow. Matusow, who occasionally entertained in night clubs by twisting pipe cleaners into animal silhouettes, was used by investigating committees as a "friendly witness" to "name" Communists. (When one has been identified as a Communist by anyone considered "friendly" to the investigating committee, he is said to have been "named." It does not matter much whether the man "named" is, in fact, a Communist. Being "named" is usually sufficient to ruin him.)

After "naming" various persons to the satisfaction of sundry investigators, Matusow declared that it had all been a hoax and that he was a fraud and a perjurer who had lied when "naming" his victims. He enjoyed testifying, liked the expense money paid to "friendly witnesses," and could not resist the publicity associated with "naming" people, he said. The Senate Internal Security Subcommittee, enraged by Matusow's reversal, spent three weeks investigating him in an effort to persuade the public that he was lying about having lied.

The most sensational investigations are usually supercharged with politics. Tradition enjoins the investigator from admitting as much and requires the investigatee to protest that he is the victim of a politically inspired character assassination. From this point most big investigations follow a predictable pattern, which, with minor variations, goes as follows:

1. The chairman begins with a pledge of steely-willed determination to get to the bottom of the skulduggery at hand, "without political fear or favor," letting heads roll where they may in the cause of justice, etc.

2. The man to be investigated announces that he is the innocent victim of a sinister political conspiracy to destroy all he stands for.

3. After opening skirmishes, the investigator announces that testimony taken to date reveals a situation so grave that it may become necessary to invite "the White House" to testify in order to "set the record straight."

4. Asked to repeat this statement for television cameras, the investigator removes his spectacles, combs

his hair, and announces that, by God, he will *demand* that "the White House" testify. This assures him of a half-minute appearance on the television network news shows during prime evening time.

5. "The White House" declares that George Washington once said that what goes on in the White House is none of Congress's business. It therefore refuses to testify.

6. The investigator laments that the White House has seen fit to obstruct an impartial inquiry. Whether its decision is motivated by devious political impulse, he declares, he will not judge.

7. At this stage the testimony of one "key witness" is found to contradict another's. The investigator observes that someone is lying, and announces that the record will be sent to the Justice Department to be studied for evidence of perjury.

8. A third witness, rumored to be so "key" that only his testimony can reveal who really warped the cue stick, sends word that he is suffering from coronary thrombosis and is forbidden by his doctors to testify.

9. What he would have said had he appeared is thereupon "leaked" to a few newspapers, provoking outraged editorial attack on the investigator's methods by all newspapers not privy to the "leak."

10. A "mystery witness" who had appeared wearing an executioner's hood to testify that the President's cousin belonged to an "apparatus" in 1935 is exposed as

a recently freed convict with a record of mail fraud and jury suborning.

11. The President's friends in Congress issue press releases declaring their intention to introduce measures that will restore fair play to the sacred investigative process.

12. Public opinion polls show a wild climb, or drop, in the investigator's political stock.

13. A simmering factional fight within the committee erupts in headlines. Each faction mourns publicly that the other has seen fit to let corrupting political considerations sully its conduct.

14. After months have passed, a news roundup on what has happened to the more famous witnesses reports one suicide, two bankruptcies, a man abandoned by his wife, another under indictment, and another selling his blood to the Red Cross for grocery money.

15. Many more months and several million words of testimony later, a foundation survey estimates that hundreds of thousands of friendships have been destroyed by arguments about whether the investigation was good or bad for the country. The committee files a divided report, noting that it will need a $200,000 appropriation for next year to continue its studies. Both factions, challenged to state what the investigation has proven, reply: "The record will speak for itself."

✻ *How to Be Investigated*

WHAT SHOULD one do if he is to be investigated?

First, he should replenish his bank account. It will cost a great deal of money living in a Washington hotel or traveling to and from the city at the pleasure of the investigators while one's normal work is suspended. Expense allowances for an investigatee, like the justice he can anticipate, are small.

A good expensive lawyer is also essential, and possibly private investigators. The lawyer should be someone with friends in the White House, Congress, and banking circles. Such lawyers get respect from investigators, while lawyers celebrated as champions of civil liberties bring out the barbarian in a congressman. Lawyers with friends in the White House, Congress, and banking circles are very expensive. Persons without much money should avoid being investigated.

Second, study your investigator. Each man has his own style; the tactics that appease one may turn another into a barracuda. Senator John L. McClellan can be positively gallant to the witness addressing his committee with deference and respect. Senator Joseph R. McCarthy treated deference and respect as tokens of frailty to be converted into passive concurrence in whatever testimony he chose to place upon the deferential tongue.

Senator Estes Kefauver returns deference with such

gentle humility that a witness is forced to grovel in return in order to avoid seeming downright arrogant.
Various witnesses have had success by being gentlemanly
with McClellan, by laughing at McCarthy, and by af-
fecting rigid dignity with Kefauver.

Third, adopt a style of defense and maintain it. Here
are some of the more common styles:

1. The Counteroffensive. This is based on the assumption that an investigation is really a battle for headlines in which victory goes to the side that beats the
other to the punch in the newsroom. The victim must
become the victimizer and try to arraign the investigators.

Howard Hughes used it successfully against the committee that tried to investigate his aircraft contracts with
the government in the mid-1940's. Before Hughes had
finished with his would-be tormentors, led by Senators
Homer Ferguson and Owen Brewster, he had successfully spread the notion that the investigation was not
motivated by solicitude for the taxpayer, but by a
desire to ruin him on behalf of a rival aircraft company.
The investigators were routed.

During the House investigation of Sherman Adams's
relationship with Bernard Goldfine in 1958, the Adams-
Goldfine side used standard public relations techniques
to upstage the investigators. Before Adams went to the
Capitol to read his statement of innocence, he read it to
television cameras at the White House. Before he took

the witness chair he had already appeared on the home screen explaining away the committee's case in reassuring prose. The coup was so successful that the investigators barely succeeded in getting their names on the networks for twenty-four hours.

Goldfine came to Washington for the show accompanied by Tex McCrary, a New York public relations expert, who tried producing Goldfine's testimony on TV film the night before he was to give it to the committee. Again, this gave the defense a monopoly on the networks next morning before the investigators could get in the first innuendo. Goldfine's counteroffensive finally failed, but his was a difficult case for any defense.

2. The Fifth Amendment. This raises problems. The investigators have worked so hard to tarnish it that relying on the Amendment is popularly interpreted as a plea of guilty. The instant a witness responds for the first time that he must decline to answer on grounds that a reply might tend to incriminate him, reporters rush to the telegraph keys with the news that he has "taken the Fifth."

In Washington jargon, "taking the Fifth" means an admission of guilt. A witness considering this defense should recognize that it will probably stigmatize him as guilty of whatever the committee wants to charge him with and probably cost him his job, always a keen source of satisfaction to a blooded investigator.

In the eyes of hearing-room habitués, claiming the Amendment's privilege is lower than the foul play the witness may hope to conceal. Washington is always willing to pump the hand of the rogue who winks openly about his misdeeds, but "taking the Fifth" is looked upon as an odious breach of good form, like bringing the town madam to the Sunday-school picnic.

Actually, the Fifth Amendment's guarantee against enforced self-incrimination is rooted in an eighteenth-century distaste for hanging a man solely on the strength of a *mea culpa* roasted out of him with red-hot tongs. Its assumption is that the police should be proficient in more than the rubber hose to earn their pay. In the rampant Communist investigations of the McCarthy era, the Amendment was denounced as a foil to the labors of patriots. McCarthy, who had the great ad man's intuitive sense for the loaded phrase, coined "Fifth Amendment Communist" to describe anyone who declined to come clean, thus stigmatizing the decliner and the Fifth Amendment in a neat, euphonious seven syllables.

The Supreme Court fortuitously aided the debasement. In 1951 the Court ruled that witnesses claiming the protection of the Amendment could not answer some questions and refuse to answer others. Witnesses planning to claim the privilege were required to assert it not only on specific questions tending to incriminate them but on all relevant questions, even though these might not lead to incrimination.

Many lawyers remained doubtful about the latitude allowed witnesses under the Court's ruling. If a witness answered a question deemed relevant by the Court, then declined to answer another, he might be subject to contempt-of-Congress prosecution. Because of the doubt, the safe course was refusal to answer any question except "Will you state your name and address?"

Men refused to give their ages, tell where they worked, identify their hobbies, give the names of their wives and children, or reveal what they had eaten for breakfast, all with the explanation that this information might tend to incriminate them. (After each refusal to answer, the witness must state in full his claim of privilege under the Fifth Amendment.)

The frustrated investigators, balked before this impenetrable defense, exacted what vengeance they could from forcing the decliners to sit for hour after hour intoning the litany over and over in reply to hundreds of prepared questions. Once a witness made it clear that he would say nothing, the investigators could abuse him a bit by making him look absurd or vicious with the peculiar questioning process.

"Why did you marry your present wife?" when answered with "I refuse to answer that question on the ground that it might tend to incriminate me," is always good for laughter at the witness's expense.

And if a man is up on suspicion of having had parlor pinks to tea in 1934, his present reputation can be nicely disposed of. Something like "In 1934, were you under direct orders from Joseph Stalin to organize a cell for the purpose of plotting the overthrow of the United States?" can make devastating reading in the home-town paper if answered with "I decline to answer that question on ground that it might tend to incriminate me."

Among "takers of the Fifth," Nathan Witt, a New York attorney, was a master stylist. Witt, whose career in the 1930's had been filled with associations in what was then called the radical left, was a constant witness in Washington in the late 1940's and early 1950's. He probably spent more time in the Senate Office Building than many senators.

Toward the end he acquired a *sang-froid* under the floodlights that many men never match in their own parlors. He would sit in the witness chair with legs crossed, gaze fixed absently on some object across the street, looking for all the world like a man waiting in a cocktail lounge to meet his wife and wondering idly whether to brace for it with a cocktail or settle for a glass of water.

The investigators would read doggedly through their piles of questions, and Witt would work them up to a deep red flush around the cheekbones by pretending to be elsewhere. After a grotesquely involved question, he might let his attention flicker momentarily over the in-terrogator, as though trying to recall where he had seen the fellow before. Then, returning his gaze to the window or studying his hands with the abstracted air of a man musing on a manicure, he would sigh: "Repeat the question please." And the investigator would toil through it again. And when he was finished, Witt would swing his crossed leg gently to and fro, as though speculating on the need for a shoeshine, and in tones conveying infinite boredom, intone: "I decline to answer on ground that it might tend to incriminate me."

If the interrogator's face was a particularly deep crimson, Witt might simply mutter in a barely audible register: "I decline to answer," knowing that the interrogator would take the bait. And the interrogator, taking it, would demand: "On what ground?" And Witt, still playing him, would murmur: "Fifth Amendment." And the interrogator, suppressing a scream, would admonish him: "Mr. Witt, you know you must give the complete statement on each response!" Then, like a schoolboy showing up a doltish teacher before the class, Witt would recite in singsong: "I must decline to answer that question on ground that it might tend to incriminate me."

Witt by this time was a *boulevardier* of the hearing rooms and so battered and buffeted by years of testifying and "taking the Fifth" that it was beyond the power of the most fanatic investigator to injure him more. His was a hard-earned *savoir-faire* for which few will care to pay the price.

3. One final defense is worth mentioning. It may be called Fun and Farce. It relies on extraneous uproar skillfully touched off just at the moment the investigators seem to be getting down to serious business. When the investigator points the first accusing finger, ideally a firecracker should explode under the chief counsel and the witness should start hitting his lawyer with a bladder.

The esence of Fun and Farce is to keep the committee distracted. If the farce runs high enough, the audience can be made to laugh, and when people start laughing at any investigation, it is in trouble. After the laughter come editorials magisterially demanding to know why Congress is lending itself to foolishness, and five hundred congressmen who thrive on calumny and libel but fear the giggle will begin urging the investigator to quiet his show down or close it.

Fun and Farce is best suited to the extrovert who suggests baffled innocence before the sophisticated intricacies of Washington. "Someone has accused me of doing bad things?" the witness's incredulous manner should convey. The witness should be able to convey this impression while rubbing a custard pie in the investigator's face

The classic performance was in an obscure investigation involving one Harry Lev. Someone will object that Lev eventually lost his fight. No matter; Justice

Holmes was often outvoted by the Supreme Court, too, but his dissents are still studied as legal classics.

The Lev investigation was chiefly concerned with a small-bore conspiracy to swindle the government on military-uniform contracts. Aside from a witness who testified from notes written in Arabic, all it ever had was Harry Lev.

It was apparent the moment Lev shambled to the witness chair that the committee was in for a desperate stand. The investigators wanted to know the secret of his company's amazing success in winning prize contracts for the manufacture of military caps. Their curiosity had been stirred by a procession of government workers responsible for the nation's military-cap supply, all of whom had profited on the side in ways exotic or financial after dealings with Harry Lev.

Lev hit his entrance cue with gusto. McClellan had scarcely settled down to it before Lev was pawing wildly through a brief case and demanding to be heard on his contributions to military headwear. Extracting a visor cap and brandishing it overhead, he declared in anguished English that his ingenuity had brought the military cap "from the horse-and-buggy to the airplane" stage of design.

Bounding from the chair, his arms suddenly filled with visor caps, he romped up to McClellan, clicked to a rusty form of attention, snapped on a cap, and saluted.

He begged the chairman to note its chic lines. While McClellan somberly worked his gavel, Lev modeled another for him, and another, and another, all the while rolling his eyeballs and urging McClellan to say where he had ever seen a handsomer cap. Before Lev returned to the witness chair he had given each senator a picture postcard showing his factory in Chicago. "I'm proud of this plant," he shouted over the uproar.

In a moment of quiet, he testified that he had emigrated from Pinsk in 1921, carrying nothing but a sewing machine, and had gone to Chicago, where he had since made a good deal of money. How much? The committee toiled to find out.

"You're a millionaire?" Senator George Bender asked him.

"I don't know anything about being a millionaire," Lev said.

Bender tried the devious approach. "You're a successful self-made man?" he asked.

"Thank you!" Lev beamed.

Bender went at him again. "You're a very rich man?" he inquired.

"I'm not a millionaire as far as character is concerned," Lev replied. Bender kept at it. Ten minutes later, Lev smiled affectionately at the senator. "Senator Bender," he said, " if you want to call me a very rich man, it's all right."

This settled, Lev resumed his autobiography. He

spoke seven languages but neither read nor wrote English, he said. Again Bender pounced. "How can you tell the difference between a hundred-dollar bill and a fifty-dollar bill?" he demanded.

With an injured look, Lev explained: "You must remember, I'm not illiterate altogether."

And so it went for the first day. Lev discoursed on the aphrodisiac qualities of turtle steak, denounced news stories depicting him as "the biggest chiseler in the world," and dashed off a check to the Treasury for $5,000 when McClellan charged him with cheating the government by that amount on a contract.

Refreshed by a night's sleep, the committee tried again next morning. Lev promptly tied them up with tales of smoked sturgeon and chicken feathers. The smoked sturgeon, he seemed to say, had been distributed at his expense to some forty government workers in the military-cap procurement business. Over a three-year period, nearly a thousand pounds of it had been purchased from Al's Fishery in Chicago. Lev delivered an ecstatic description of Al's smoked sturgeon, but the senators cut him off with the ugly suggestion that hundreds of pounds of it had been shipped around the country as gifts to influence government workers.

Lev was indignant. "A gift," he declared, "is something a person wears."

What about those free caps he had given to officers working in military procurement?

"I remember it just like it was a dream," Lev replied.

How many had he passed out?

He shrugged. "To me, a cap amounts to as much as the ashes of a cigarette."

The interrogation lurched onward until, for a few sane moments, it finally seemed to be forming a constricting circle of incrimination. Just as the committee stood on the threshold of success, Lev sat bolt upright and announced in thundering tones: "Everybody is conversed with Bible!"

Senatorial jaws went slack at this gratuitous irrelevancy, and Lev plunged ahead, taking advantage of the politician's instinctive fear of showing snappishness about Scripture. Lev began telling them about David. After David had become a king, he related, he kept his shepherd's horn hanging always "on the palace wall." "Why?" Lev asked rhetorically. "Because in case his mind is going to run away with him he would not forget his lowly beginnings!"

At this, Lev leaped from the chair, stood glowering at the committee, and thrust his right arm upward toward the chandelier. Glistening on his extended middle finger was a silver thimble.

"This is where I started!" he cried. "With a thimble! This is my horn that reminds me where I come from!" When feeling excessive pride about his rise from Pinsk to Chicago, he went on, it was his custom to go listen to his thimble, which told him: "Calm down, calm down."

"Calm down!" McClellan ordered.

"You're not trying to be a clown here to avoid telling the committee the truth, are you?" asked Senator Stuart Symington.

"No siree!" said Lev.

By the following day, senatorial nerves were fraying. Lev accused the committee of persecuting the Army Quartermaster Corps. Records suggesting that he had bilked the government of $26,000 on cap contracts were merely evidence of sloppy office work in his plant, he said.

"I'm learning more about how the disefficiency my office is," he marveled when the records were produced.

What about those letters from competitive firms stating that they had never received the privileges that the procurement officers—recipients of Al's smoked sturgeon—had accorded Lev?

"I got an awful lot of enemies," Lev confided. "My competition, they love to see me being in the grave." He had never given "a broken cent" for special favor, he insisted.

"Stinky deals," rumbled Bender, now near apoplexy.

"The grossest inefficiency," sorrowed McClellan. Or worse, "finagling" the government.

Lev was outraged. Had his only thought not been

for the nation's servicemen? Had he not proved it by giving the government special rights to Lev cap patents? And why?

"For the reason why I like to see the servicemen having a good appearance," he said.

Next day the groggy investigators plodded onward. For hour upon hour they promised to have him up for perjury, they bombarded him with angry questions, they accused him of bribery, cheating, "fixing."

Bender finally exploded. "You evade!" he roared from the depths of his frustration. "You hesitate! You delay! You procrastinate! You can equivocate! You can repeat questions! You can fix! You can do everything except give a direct answer! You're a very clever man!"

A radiance of delight lit Lev's face. "You think so?" he asked triumphantly.

In the end, Bender, in a bellowing rage, went too far. He accused Lev of making "shoddy" hats for the Navy.

His patriotism impugned, Lev furiously wagged his finger at Bender and declared: "I deserve at least from the committee I should get a Congressional Medal! Never mind accusing my workmanship!"

On this note the committee folded its hand. Its final act was to send the record to the Internal Revenue Service. After months of struggle, it was decoded and sent to the courts, where it proved helpful in convicting Lev for conspiracy to defraud the government and bribery. And so, in the end, Lev lost, but not without leaving a monumental proof that the tormented can at least work vengeance upon his congressional tormentors.

✳ *The Question*

ARE CONGRESSIONAL investigations good or bad?

The congressional investigating power is good. Some improvement in congressional investigators would be fine.

9

The Tattlers

ONCE UPON A TIME the newspaperman found assuagement for his ego and compensation for his miserable salary in the notion that he was a free soul who talked back to police captains and licked no man's spats. Only a fragment of the myth lingers today among the 1,300 reporters composing the Washington "press corps." Here the American journalist has realized his ancient yearning for respectability, forced the publisher to pay him as much as the printers, and banded into clubs and trade societies for which, like the dentist and

192

veterinarian, he writes learned articles brooding about what he calls his "profession."

Many belong to country clubs, play golf, invest in the stock market, compete with hostesses to lure politicians to their houses, and otherwise behave like grocery-chain vice-presidents. As practicing members of the bourgeoisie, they tend to take their trade very seriously. In his Potomac manifestation, the reporter has become The Washington Correspondent. It is his conviction that he is no longer just an inky tattletale, but a statesman, or in Douglass Cater's phrase, a member of "the fourth branch of government."

Harboring such fancies, the newspaperman may conceive himself an important man and expect a certain deference. When offended or aroused—and he offends and arouses easily—he may quickly become dangerous. Relaxing socially, he may be inflated by being urged to expatiate on what the President has done wrong lately, how the Republicans can win the next election, or what is needed in the way of foreign-policy innovation.

One should not burden him with one's own views. He spends his days listening in silent agony to wretches and wise men, and he wishes that everyone would listen, for a change, to what he has to say.

Structurally, the press corps is an elaborate society within a society, with its own well-defined caste system. At its most exalted level stand the celebrated columnists and radio-television "personalities," men as august as

Popes and with more prerogatives than justices of the Supreme Court. At the bottom is the vast dirty-fingernail set, the infantrymen who man dozens of dreary outposts waiting for something to flare and ready to contain it until reinforcements arrive. In between are hordes of specialists—men who keep track of the President's diet, women who cover cocktail parties, men who are received by the Vice-President, investigators, agricultural specialists, people who understand nuclear physics, labor law, Treasury notes, and writs of certiorari, men who can talk man to man with admirals and senators, with social workers, Chief Justices, and ambassadors.

Each day the battalions infiltrate the government to find "news." Because "news" is often the very stuff that government wants to keep secret, an intricate government defense system has been developed to frustrate the newsmen. In the bureaucracy the command post of the defense operation is called the "public information office," and its agents, "press officers." The chief mission of the "public information office" is to see that the public gets no information except what the government wants it to have. This is information depicting the government as noble, sagacious, and farsighted.

The reporter discovers that the last place in Washington to get information is at the "public information office." Instead, he pokes into unexplored corridors badgering government workers less skilled in duplicity.

Canny "press officers" seek to prevent this by warning the workers to say nothing when the reporters call and to refer them back to the "public information office."

A few years ago the Defense Department issued a directive epitomizing the government attitude toward "public information." It stated that no information was to become public unless it made a "constructive contribution" to the Pentagon's "mission." In English, this meant: "Nothing gets out unless it makes us look good." Philip J. Farley, while working as a special State Department adviser on disarmament, told a reporter seeking information: "I realize, of course, that a free press is the bulwark of a democracy, but it is very difficult conducting the affairs of government when things appear in the newspapers."

Unhappily for the government, the reporters have natural advantages over the "press officers" which make it easy to penetrate their clumsy blockades. The State Department may, for example, enforce silence within its own precincts on the stupendous news that A. Addison Anderson is to be appointed Ambassador to London, but it cannot stop members of the Senate Foreign Relations Committee from talking, or suppress the cocktail nattering of Mrs. Anderson, or stop Anderson's tailor from telling a friend that the old boy is being fitted for knee breeches.

The press, with its highly flexible attack force, has ears planted among members of the Foreign Relations

Committee, at cocktail parties attended by Mrs. Anderson, and, sometimes, even at the elbow of Anderson's tailor's friend. Indeed, the "press officer's" defeat is so certain at every turn that if his task were less loathsome it would be possible to pity him.

The flexibility of the attack against him derives from the diversity of the press society. At its base are the wire services—Associated Press and United Press International—supplying manpower to monitor every possible news forum of government. These are the vacuum-cleaner boys, who scoop up everything in sight and funnel it into their offices for relay around Washington by teletype. Much of it is junk, the effluvium of the government mimeograph which flows through Washington night and day. The "wire man's" task is to collect it and process it for dead-pan transmission on the teletype.

In the social order of the press corps, he is low man, but without him the mighty would be impotent, for he supplies the raw material of which syndicated columns and television scripts are woven. He is always out there on the front lines, watching the faces and listening to the talk, ruining his arches and wearing out his hams, to get the story on the spot. Over the years he grows into the scenery of the place to which he is assigned. It is his curse that the sterile format in which he must write prevents him from telling more than a fraction of what he knows, for about his own narrow fragment of Washington he usually knows more than the most celebrated pundit writing what purports to be the "inside story" of his beat. Generally, he acquires the sad, tired look characteristic of the combat man who has learned to take the professional view of battle, knowing that the generals will get the glory if he performs well.

After the wire men comes a profusion of reporters working for individual papers, networks, news syndicates, and trade journals. These men concentrate on specific "beats," thus duplicating much of the work of the "wires," but looking for special "angles" to suit their peculiar audiences. The television man hunts for the story that can be photographed. The others, called "pencil reporters" by the TV men, claim higher caste than the wires because they limit themselves to developing only the stories that interest them, passing up the bales of junk that the poor wire man must process.

In this set distinctions proliferate. To be worked successfully, each beat requires its own set of human traits, and this makes for differences among the types of reporters scattered in pressrooms across Washington. The White House, for example, is the dullest beat in Washington, yet the glamour associated with it makes it one of the choicest plums in the trade. In Washington this glamour consists of sitting most of the day in a windowless lobby isolated from everyone who is running the government and waiting for the White House Press Secretary to distribute press releases.

For the wire service reporters there is a certain excitement in the foot race over waxed floors to win a two-second advantage on the telephone. Merriman Smith, of UPI, once fractured his clavicle in the contest. Otherwise, it is a sedentary job, consisting largely of reading paperbacks or playing poker and fan-tan in the pressroom. In short, the ideal assignment for a rheumatic veteran. What one finds, however, is not a crowd of sedate elders, but a boisterous gang that enjoys racing over mountain passes at eighty miles an hour, putting catsup into provincial slot machines, and otherwise behaving like the Lafayette Escadrille on a Paris furlough. The atmosphere is infectious even for the staid, who may find themselves bawling ribald doggerel in the plush saloons of distant cities while idling away the hours of a presidential vacation. The myth that the White House is a glamorous beat impels the men who work it to behave as they conceive glamorous reporters must.

Other beats imprint their personalities just as indelibly. The State Department reporter quickly learns to talk like a fuddy-duddy and to look grave, important, and inscrutable. The Pentagon man always seems to have just come in off maneuvers. The Capitol reporter eschews the raucous spirit of the White House and affects the hooded expression of the man privy to many important deals. Like the politicians he covers, he tends to garrulity, coarse jokes, and bourbon and learns to hate reform. The Treasury man dismisses as dubious all that cannot be statistically proved; the labor specialist affects the blunt speech of the working stiff; the society reporter flutters and clucks; and the science specialist becomes detached and takes up pipe smoking.

At the apex of the society stand the lordly Brahmans, the high priests to whom great men look anxiously for omens of approbation or disfavor. The caste falls broadly into three orders: syndicated columnists, bureau chieftains, and network commentators. Theirs is all that remains of the tradition of personal journalism, for it is their highest prerogative, taboo to all others in the "corps," to put their own opinions before the public.

This gives them an immense advantage over their lesser colleagues. Suppose that the Secretary of Defense decides to abolish the Army because the Treasury believes it is too expensive. He will issue a press release stating that the Army is being abolished in order to improve the over-all national defense. Run-of-the-mine reporters are required by the code of their trade to report this fiction at its face value. They must write: "The Secretary of Defense announced today that the Army will be abolished to strengthen the over-all national defense." This is known in the trade as "objective reporting," and is highly revered.

The Brahmans are confounded by no such nonsense. One may write: "The Secretary of Defense stooped to a new low in hypocrisy in his flimsy attempt to justify abolishing the Army. In fact, this decision was dictated by the big banking interests, which are now running the Treasury and are willing to imperil the national security to get tax reductions this year."

Senators in search of an opinion may plagiarize the Brahman's and start a debate at the Capitol. The next day another Brahman may counter as follows: "As usual, the hidden enemies of democracy were quick to order their stooges in press and government to start smearing that dedicated patriot, the Secretary of Defense. The pretext was his order, secretly drafted by the previous Administration, to do what courage has long dictated, and abolish the Army. Unpublished documents demonstrate that the Army, in fact, has been obsolete for the past five years. . . ."

Thus another debate is under way, with the Brahmans in the vanguard. Obviously Brahmans are important to the government. They may be deadly to the man they oppose en masse. Fortunately for Presidents, congressmen, Cabinet, *et al.*, the caste is riven with jealousies and diversity of view, guaranteeing that they will rarely stand en bloc on any issue of public policy.

Still, the canny officeholder works to please them. When the lowly reporter comes calling, the great man may have a flunky reroute him to the "public information office." When the Brahman knocks, the statesman is all teeth and charm. The reporter is a tool to be used when convenient or a nuisance to be brushed aside when he bars the path. The Brahman is a man to be had to tea or dinner or a weekend under sail.

* *The White House News Conference*

THE WHITE HOUSE news conference is a highly stylized public ritual that follows rigid procedures and a protocol almost as inflexible as court etiquette under Louis XIV. From the reporter's viewpoint it is essentially a television performance, and the sensible place to cover it, for most journalistic purposes, is from a television set in the office.

When the performance is "live" on television, most reporters assigned to cover the story do, in fact, work from the office TV screen if they are close to deadlines. Yet attendance at President Kennedy's shows is often double that at President Eisenhower's, when the working reporters had to be present. What accounts for the increase? Some comparisons between the Kennedy and Eisenhower formats may be in order.

If you were a reporter with a question you wanted to take up with President Eisenhower, you appeared thirty minutes before the appointed hour outside the Indian Treaty Room on the fourth floor of the Executive Office Building, across the street from the White House, and took your place in a queue of about two hundred others.

Not all of these were working reporters. Some were visiting newspaper executives come to see the spectacle, and others were social-minded correspondents who found this a smart place to meet their colleagues. Others were there simply to look at the President so that they could speculate about his psyche on the evidence of their eyes. Others had come out of more complicated motives not entirely free of crass self-interest, for in Eisenhower's day the correspondent could hope to share equal status with the President in the performance.

This was possible because the rules of the news conference required each questioner to begin by identifying himself by name and organization. Thus, the television film of the event and *The New York Times* transcript published next day offered tempting devices for the ambitious reporter to let the world know that he was the important kind of chap who talked to Presidents.

Now, imagine that you were a reporter determined to raise a question at the Eisenhower news conference of not so long ago:

As you file into the room, you show your credentials to a couple of armed gentlemen and look for a seat. It will be helpful if you are a midget, for the Indian Treaty Room is too small for the audience, and to accommodate it the overseers allow only six inches between each row of chairs. You fit yourself in by pushing the reportorial buttocks far to the back of the seat and digging your knees firmly into the kidneys of the fellow in front of you. Your elbows will be pinned against your pelvis by the equally cramped gentlemen on either side, and, if it is a warm day, when the television lights come on, you will begin to appreciate how it was in the Black Hole of Calcutta.

Locked into position and basting in your own perspiration, you are ready to raise your question with Eisenhower. The first problem is to get the floor. This is done by standing up, looking Eisenhower dead in the eye, calling "Mr. President!" and waiting for him to give you a nodding signal to start talking. Your chances of succeeding are only slightly better than a bleeding man's of swimming unmolested through a field of sharks. To begin with, there are at least twenty other persons to whom recognition is a question of bread for the kiddies. The following are a few representative types. Note them well, for, after mutation to equip them for survival in somewhat different conditions, they will appear later in the Kennedy era to compound your troubles:

The Television Network Reporter. His network is headed by important men who assume as a matter of course that their White House agent commands the presidential ear. Moreover, they have cameras present to prove it, and they intend to on their news shows that night. His network intends to say on its news show that evening: "Our man, Chazz Goadly, asked the President today about unrest in Kurdistan," then cut in with film showing him asking. If the television reporter fails to get recognized for many weeks in succession, he will soon be replaced by a television man with more moxie.

Because there are four TV news services represented in the room and two wire-service men, who also must ask questions, a large part of the usual thirty minutes is pre-empted in advance by men of tigerish determination and immense skill at getting in ahead of you.

The Ham. This gentleman may represent anybody. He is recognizable by his blue shirt. Somebody once told him that blue was telegenic, and he is hell-bent on getting himself televised while advising the President how to manage the government. For this reason, his question will be an extended speech followed by a request for "comment on that."

Being a ham, he has an inborn genius for commanding the President's attention and will block you out every time. His favorite tactic is bobbing and weaving. He pops to his feet, jack-in-the-box fashion, while the President is still discussing the previous question, and begins to bob and weave like a middleweight hoping to stay four rounds with Floyd Patterson. This distracts the President and puts a lien on his attention, whereupon the ham then comes out with a commandingly theatrical and undeniable "Mr. President!"

The Important Personage. This is the mighty columnist or the famous bureau chieftain with a big reputation for somber thinking. This reputation needs frequent sustenance with a recondite question posed to the President before an audience of his inferiors. Usually he is a Brahman of the press corps, and the sheer awe inspired by his presence keeps the television man, the ham, and the dirty-fingernail types in their seats while he stands and lets his dignity reach out toward the President.

The Hustler. This is the fellow who services a string of small papers in the Gadsden Purchase. His chief mission in life is keeping his name in the public eye. The television camera affords him this opportunity. It makes little difference what he asks the President or whether the President thinks it worth answering. The important thing is recognition. If he services remote and impecunious papers, he may seek to flatter a subscriber by challenging the President for an opinion on the sewerage-system referendum in Schlamiel County, where he has a client.

All the foregoing ladies and gentlemen, you will find, are masters of the press conference, who have spent years perfecting techniques for getting recognized. The indispensable quality for success, however, is timing. Despite changes made by Kennedy, timing is still quintessential. First, there must be an inner sense of when the President is about to finish answering the previous question. As soon as his instinct tells him the President is about to end, the reporter must shoot to his feet, preferably in a faintly aggressive movement calculated to startle the President into noticing him. At the same time the lips must be parted and the "Mr. President!" already silently formed and ready for launching the instant the President finishes his sentence.

Even then it can be a close thing. A dozen or so competitors, equally skilled and equally determined, will be on their feet simultaneously, using the techniques that have won for them over the years. This is no place for the beginner unless he comes resigned to a long and arduous course of training which may not pay off in recognition until his middle age.

Under Eisenhower, after the President had sprayed the air with a shotgun load of questions about a great many matters without developing any of them in coherent form, the senior White House correspondent roared: "Thank you, Mr. President!" and the thunder of stampeding feet was heard, followed by the crash of massed bodies through the rear door as the reporters went for their telephones.

The correspondents with late deadlines drifted off in packs to sit down over coffee and puzzle out what the President really meant. Because of the way the news conference had developed, it was often hard to tell.

Coherent development of a single subject was virtually impossible with the helter-skelter system under which the questions were submitted. Many reporters came with questions already written out or fixed in mind. Rarely were two questions asked on the same subject, except on the more dramatic occasions. The supplementary question, the essence of the House of Commons question hour, with which the news conference is often compared, was virtually unknown. Trying to frame it in the atmosphere of the Eisenhower news conference was like trying to compose a sonnet under machine-gun fire.

When President Kennedy took over he made two changes that dealt terrible blows to correspondents' status. First, he decided to do many of his news conferences "live." (Under Eisenhower there had been only film, which might or might not be shown someplace, later.) "Live" television inevitably diminished the reporter, for the story, which it had been his prerogative to give first to the world under the old system, was now relayed directly by the President while the reporter sat imprisoned in the conference room, little more than a stage prop for Kennedy's performance.

At first there appeared to be some compensation for the loss of stature. "Live" television, with its guaranteed mass audience, promised a tremendous new breadth of exposure for the status striver. Kennedy ruthlessly foreclosed this glory for the hams by decreeing that reporters should no longer announce their names and organizations. The blow was cruel. Now the correspondent confronting the President was merely a face in a crowd on television, and the printed record dismissed him as the anonymous "Q."

There was a third change. Kennedy took the conference out of the old Indian Treaty Room and relocated it in the spacious, air-conditioned, modern auditorium of the State Department Building. This not only created a more pleasing TV setting but freed the cameras, which had been frozen in the back of the room in the old setting, and permitted additional views from the front and side of the hall.

Telegenically, Eisenhower's news conference looked antique in comparison. Kennedy's also forced some new adjustments on the press. Imagine that you are a reporter assigned to deal with the Kennedy conference in its "live" manifestation. If you are close to a deadline, you simply stay away. You sit by the office TV screen, where you can compose and transmit a story while the President is still talking. Suppose, however, that you decide to attend with a question for the President. You stroll through the theatrical lobby of the State Department auditorium, present your credentials to the inevitable armed gentlemen at the door, and are admitted without delay.

Once inside you have the sensation of entering a theater balcony from the rear. You select a comfortable and spacious cushioned seat to suit your purpose. If you favor your right profile you sit on the left side of the house, and vice versa, because the camera shots of the reporters are usually made from the front positions farthest from the questioner.

If you want to be recognized, you sit as far down

front as possible, because you may later have to shout down several competitors for recognition and reporters in the back are easily drowned out in the din. There are dozens of other considerations involved in selecting a seat. James M. Cannon, of *Newsweek,* has given one of the more whimsical.

When he was first transferred from New York to Washington, he has explained, it occurred to him that the news conference might offer the ideal method for notifying many friends quickly of the shift. He reported to the auditorium and studied the ground with his problem in mind. The location whence he was most likely to be televised without asking a question, he reasoned, would be one near a man with a consistent record for getting recognized. Moreover, he figured, the longer the question, the more likely the chance that he would be spotted in the background by his acquaintances. Therefore, he should situate himself near someone likely to ask a lengthy question. A student of news-conference transcripts, he reasoned that Edward P. Morgan, of the American Broadcasting Company, was not only likely to be recognized by the President but would also probably have the longest question of the day.

Accordingly, he took a seat behind and slightly to one side of Morgan, so that he would not be blocked from the picture when Morgan stood and the camera zoomed in. His strategy proved perfect, and within a few days he received notes from various friends around the country expressing surprise to find him in Washington.

What the Kennedy news conference gained in comfort it has lost in intimacy. The loss creates a new problem for the man struggling to catch the President's eye. Interestingly, there has been no noticeable decrease in the number of determined competitors for the President's attention. Indeed, the bigger crowds attracted by the size and comfort of the auditorium also seem to include more people impotent to resist the compulsion to perform. Because of the hall's great size and because of the increased competition, it is no longer enough to get the President's eye in recognition. You must also have the vocal cords of a hog caller.

When the President nods toward one man among perhaps thirty shouting from the remote vastness of the auditorium, the signal may be interpreted by several that each has been granted the floor. Accordingly, three or four voices may start bellowing questions simultaneously. When caught in one of these shouting matches, you must roar out ruthlessly, drowning all opposition, refusing to yield a syllable until all others have been silenced. The man without vocal stamina is a poor survival risk.

There is one saddening development of the "live" news conference. The old thunder of massed bodies crashing against the exits in competition to be first out of the room with the story is no more. In the old days this put a completely satisfying exclamation point of sound to the end of the news conference. With the "live" format, there is no reason for it. By the time the President is finished the wire services are usually finishing their own accounts of the meeting, which have been written by men who stayed by the office screen.

Nowadays the reporters troop out quietly, like so many spear carriers trudging off the set after the show is over.

✳ *Hindsighting and Crystal-Balling*

ONE OF the principal duties of the Washington press corps is to master the twin arts of Hindsighting and Crystal-Balling. Many of the city's most prominent journalists work at little else. The enjoyment of these skills is not, however, something that is limited to newspapermen. Practically all Washingtonians dabble in both. Indeed, it is mandatory upon anyone hoping to achieve the mildest degree of status to practice both with professional finesse. With a little application almost anyone can become proficient enough in both Hindsighting and Crystal-Balling to impress a congressman.

There are two basic rules of Crystal-Balling, and it is absolutely essential that they never be violated:

1. Always predict that something *will* happen; never predict that something will *not* happen.

2. Preface every prediction with a qualifying "if" or "unless."

A third rule, especially helpful for advanced Crystal-Balling, is: Predict the improbable.

To illustrate application of the basic rules, consider the political situation following President Eisenhower's heart attack of 1955, one year before the presidential election. Many of Washington's most skilled Crystal-Ballers ignored the first rule by predicting: "Eisenhower will not run for a second term." When Eisenhower ran for a second term, their reputations were tarnished. If you predict that something will not happen, whereupon it happens, you are utterly defenseless. Moreover, in a city where the improbable occurs twelve times a day, it is foolhardy to predict that anything will not occur.

Now, suppose that you had remembered the rules when others were blithely ignoring them. Within the great latitude they allow, you might have said: "Eisenhower *will run* for a second term (Rule 1: predict the positive) despite his heart attack *if* (Rule 2: use a qualifier) he is satisfied that his recovery is satisfactory."

Consider the beauty of this prediction, which, under the circumstances, was the only possible one the truly finished Crystal-Baller could have produced. First, it is positive: "Eisenhower will run." Second, it is improbable. With the experts predicting that he will not run, it will be laughed away and forgotten. However, if Eisenhower does later decide to run, someone will inevitably recall that you predicted it and articles about your prescience will appear in the papers. You will receive local and perhaps national tribute as a soothsayer and may even be asked to write a syndicated column on politics.

Third, you have safely hedged the prediction with "if he is satisfied," et cetera. If he later decides not to run and someone recalls your prediction that he would run, you merely have to take cover under your vague "if" clause.

The only man in Washington who kept his head and remembered the rules after Eisenhower's heart attack was Leonard Hall, the Republican National Chairman. When Eisenhower did decide to run, Hall was hailed as an oracle of the first magnitude. In 1948, one of the few to predict Truman's victory was Leslie Biffle. Ten years later he was still celebrated in Washington as a seer par excellence.

Suppose, however, that you were too timid to gamble for the big stakes as Hall did, and wanted merely to ride along safely with the crowd forecasting that Eisenhower would not run. You would not say: "Eisenhower will not run for a second term." (Rule 1: never predict that something will *not* happen.)

Instead, you would submerge the negative in a positive and skillfully qualified prediction. For example: "Nixon will get the 1956 Republican presidential nomination by acclamation *unless* (Rule 2: use a qualifier) a dark-horse candidate appears at the last minute."

Notice that you have not become involved in the question whether Eisenhower will run again, but have finessed it nicely by moving on into fields of advanced prescience. If Eisenhower does decide to run again, it is highly unlikely that anyone in the excitement will recall your forecast about Nixon and dark horses. If someone does, you have a simple escape. You shrug and reply: "But that was based on the hypothesis that Eisenhower might not run. It was always obvious, of course, that he would, but I was concerned with what might happen if he did the unexpected."

But—suppose Eisenhower had refused to run. You would have been in business on the grand scale. Given Nixon's following in the Republican rank and file, plus Eisenhower's natural reluctance to interfere in Republican politics, Nixon is a sure bet to get the nomination by acclamation, thus insuring you a reputation for omniscience that will be talked about in the embassies. If Nixon fails to win it by acclamation, or if he loses it, you are still safe, thanks to your skillful application of Rule 2.

In the circumstances, any other contender for the nomination is "a dark-horse candidate." And so if someone objects that you wrongly predicted that Nixon would win by acclamation, you simply point to your qualifying clause: "unless a dark-horse candidate appears at the last minute."

Hindsighting is even easier than Crystal-Balling. There is only one basic rule: Be provocative.

First, however, what is Hindsighting? Hindsighting

is the art of explaining why political events happened. Though distinguished universities teach the young something called political science, there is no more science in getting elected than there is in the smile of the Mona Lisa.

Getting elected is more akin to art than to science. No politician can say with truth why he got elected or why he lost. He is like a painter or a writer or a composer of music in the uncertainty of his reception. He must affect the glands of the reviewers the right way. He must be lucky in his timing. A performance that the reviewers might have hailed yesterday as a masterpiece can get deadly notices if given on a day when too many of them are dyspeptic or cross at their wives.

It is impossible to say beyond contradiction what this or that politician did right or wrong and why the vote turned this way or that. In Washington, however, there is an eternal effort to explain precisely these questions and solve the enigma of the voter. The Hindsighter, then, is the man who explains why it happened. Since no one can be sure why it happened, everyone can be a Hindsighter, and is.

Of course, in a community where everyone is Hindsighting it is not enough to give obvious explanations for the event under discussion. The explanation, remember, must be provocative.

A medical man may open a cadaver, count its ribs, and conclude that the human body has twenty-four ribs. For a Hindsighter, it is not enough to go to the 1956 election returns, count the vote, and conclude that Eisenhower beat Stevenson because he received ten million more votes. The Hindsighter must explore the mystery of why Eisenhower got ten million more votes than Stevenson. The medical scientist does not waste his time worrying why the Almighty saw fit to stock the cadaver with twenty-four ribs; however, the Hindsighter is not a scientist, but a dilettante on the fringe of the political art.

Celebrated Hindsighters usually assign multiple causes for events. Putting provocative explanations into bemusing combination is the art in its highest form, and apprentice Hindsighters must expect to do a lot of field work before operating at this level. Nevertheless, the possible explanations for any political event are so numerous that even the completely untutored may participate with considerable proficiency.

By way of example, let us review a small sample of the reasons given by advanced Hindsighters for Stevenson's 1956 defeat. Whole books will be written explaining Nixon's hairbreadth loss to Kennedy in 1960, but note the variety of reasons that may be conceived for an event as simple as Eisenhower's crushing of Stevenson. Memorize a half dozen explanations, for they will come in handy if you are confronted by a representative of the League of Women Voters over cocktails.

Stevenson lost because he was a divorced man and offended the women's vote,

Because he made jokes and offended the serious vote,

Because he looked nervous on television and offended the Dave Garroway vote,

Because he used high-flown words and offended the lowbrow vote,

Because he lacked a broad smile and offended the happy vote,

Because he talked with a cultivated accent and offended the land-grant-college vote,

Because he had a weak arm wave and offended the hairy-chested vote,

Because he worked past newspaper deadlines on his speech drafts and offended the press vote.

And, because he endorsed a nuclear test ban, because he proposed abolishing the draft, because the Israelis invaded Egypt, because his 1952 campaign style was not used in 1956, because he suggested on election eve that Eisenhower might have another heart attack.

And, because Truman campaigned for him, because Estes Kefauver failed to win the farm vote, because labor failed to deliver for him, because the Democratic congressional leaders preferred a Republican President and quit working for him.

And, because he was weak on civil rights and lost the Negro vote,

Because he was not against the Supreme Court and lost the South,

Because the suburbanization of the country had transformed all the Democratic city dwellers into middle-class Republicans, et cetera.

Distinguished Hindsighters would never use all these explanations for his defeat. They would pick four or five, more or less at random, but usually on the basis of their own abilities to extemporize at length on esoteric aspects of each, then weave them into a persuasive tapestry.

The beginner may select a few causes on which he can discourse with relative fluency, and practice them on spouse or friends to get the feel of it. Confidence may be acquired in a few test runs at crowded cocktail parties, preferably with persons you expect never to see again.

Next the beginner will want to start practicing "Projection," for this is the ultimate goal of Hindsighting. "Projection" is the process of taking your explanations of why, say, Stevenson lost in 1956 and projecting them into the process of Crystal-Balling the next campaign.

If on the eve of the 1960 Democratic Convention, for example, one has expounded the theory that Stevenson lost because he offended the land-grant-college vote by talking with a refined accent, he might go on to deduce that Kennedy would be a dangerously risky nominee because he speaks with a refined accent. Conversely, if you have elucidated the thesis that Stevenson looked nervous on television, you may deduce that Kennedy would be an excellent Democratic nominee because he is exceedingly telegenic.

This, in fact, is exactly what the professional politicians do when they sit down to choose a candidate. The difference is that these gentlemen check out every one of a thousand-odd explanations of why Kennedy can and cannot win, strike some sort of crude balance sheet, then listen to what their stomachs tell them.

* *Esoterica*

LIKE CONGRESS and the bureaucracy, the Washington press corps has its own argot. Following are explanations for some of the more common terms:

1. *The National Press Club.* This is an institution composed largely of lobbyists, public relations men, and businessmen. It is notable for a splendid stag bar where a genuine Washington correspondent—but rarely a Brahman—may occasionally be found at ease among the ad men. Newspapermen are eligible for membership at a reduced rate of eighty dollars per year and may use the bars and dining room when space is open. By quaint custom, only press members may vote for club officers. Though the newspapermen fancy themselves one of the democratic system's ultimate bulwarks, the elections are rigorously controlled and rigged years in advance by an

autocratic political machine. As in most totalitarian states, there is rarely more than one candidate for President. Brahmans normally avoid the club as a low-status symbol and seek membership in more exclusive establishments.

2. *The Gridiron Club.* This is an eating society whose membership is limited to fifty men, usually Brahmans. Each spring it serves one fine meal to which every officeholder of any importance is invited. As with the White House, its invitations amount to commands. The Gridiron did not take it well when President Eisenhower began rejecting invitations. "We don't want him anyhow," said one venerable Gridironer after the second refusal. During the dinner the members present a series of skits lampooning their most honored guests. The wit is broad and rarely barbed enough to give offense. Harold Ickes, a master at giving offense, dismissed it as "dull." Nevertheless, because of its glittering guest list, the dinner is a first-priority target for every lobbyist in the country. In 1955 a lobbyist was fired because he failed to get tickets for a client.

3. *The "leak."* The leak is any exciting news that someone in government surreptitiously slips to a reporter or two. It makes all reporters not privy to the leak very exasperated because it results in their getting "beaten." Sometimes leaks are calculated. Someone who has a dirty piece of news he wants to plant, and who is

220

sensitive about being recognized as the source, may slip it to a friendly reporter.

Other times the leak is a simple act of friendship. A public man who likes a reporter or owes him a favor may reward him with a choice bit of news as a token of esteem. One of the most famous leaks of the 1950's was the work of Attorney General Herbert Brownell, who met with a select group of reporters one evening to inform them that Earl Warren was to be appointed Chief Justice. Actually, like amour inside hospitals, there is much less leaking than all the talk about it would suggest.

When a reporter is beaten by his competitor, his defense is often to denigrate the opposition's enterprise by charging that the story was leaked. A lot of leaks are really "exclusives" won by ingenuity and enterprise.

4. *The "exclusive."* This is what moviegoers know as the "scoop," and is the badge of excellence in the trade. It is the story that no other reporter has. There are many kinds of exclusives. The garden variety reveal minor bureaucratic appointments, personal feuds in Congress, new nuances of thinking in the State Department, and such low-grade stuff.

The more important exclusives are stories dragged out of a reluctant government by ingenuity, courage, and persistence. Unhappily for the newsman, the age of instantaneous communications has destroyed the economic value of the exclusive. Nowadays, when the exclusive is printed or broadcast it can be quickly duplicated and placed in general circulation through press agencies, networks, and competing newspapers, thus diminishing its economic value to the organization that produced it. It is chiefly prized today for its cachet within the trade. A really good exclusive may also earn the reporter a small financial bonus through one of the many foundation prizes for "distinguished reporting," which are usually awarded for each year's most interesting exclusives.

5. *The "backgrounder."* This is a private news conference. Admission is by invitation only. (In a news conference anyone with a press card may participate.) Backgrounders usually take place in private homes or over meals in private dining rooms. The reporters attend under an agreement that they will not attribute any information they may get to the man who supplies it. Instead, they attribute it to "unimpeachable sources," "government officials," "the highest authority," and such disembodied oracles.

Hidden in anonymity, the government man may say almost anything he pleases without being held accountable for it, though everyone who cares may quickly learn where it originated. Occasionally the reporters find their informant publicly denying what, as "an unimpeachable source," he has urged them to proclaim.

Edwin A. Lahey, the veteran correspondent for the Knight newspapers, has given the most succinct definition of the backgrounder. "Washington," he explains, "is so vast that substitutes are found for getting information. One of them is the institution called the background dinner or background luncheon. It's a wonderful device for impressing your home office that you know a lot of big guys. You put $20 on your expense account for having dinner with the Secretary of the Treasury. This impresses the city editor, and he never thinks to ask what you get for your $20. And here's what you get for your $20: either a boring couple of hours listening to what the man wants to tell you, or in some cases you get . . . viciously and cruelly victimized."

Every reporter can cite a few personal cases of victimization. There was a classic instance in early 1953 when the late John Foster Dulles completed his first official tour of Western European capitals. In a backgrounder he told American correspondents that he had been warning the European allies that this country would undertake its "agonizing reappraisal" unless the European Defense Community became an approaching reality within ninety days. The reporters who printed this as gospel were left holding the bag when Dulles, two days later, blithely insisted that he had never said any such thing in Europe. His purpose—to throw a scare into the Western European leaders—had been served without substantive action, and the reporters privy to the backgrounder had been made to look thoroughly incompetent.

6. *The "one-party press."* The Democrats have been proved correct in their observation that the American press is predominantly under Republican management. In 1960, 731 papers endorsed the Republican, Nixon; only 208 backed the Democrat, Kennedy. In more significant terms, papers supporting Nixon had 70.9 per cent of the country's newspaper circulation; those supporting Kennedy had 15.8 per cent.

The circulation spread in 1944 was 68 per cent Republican, 18 per cent Democratic; in 1948, 78 per cent Republican, 10 per cent Democratic; in 1952, 80 per cent Republican, 11 per cent Democratic; in 1956, 72 per cent Republican, 13 per cent Democratic.

Nevertheless, publishers occasionally complain that their news pages are dominated by Democratic-biased Washington reporters. Late in the 1960 campaign, Nixon met in New York with an intimate group of political confidants and a few publishing tycoons. The talk turned to press coverage of the Nixon campaign.

There were complaints that despite the overwhelming editorial support for Mr. Nixon the reporters were manipulating their coverage against him. A publisher present spoke up to complain that the reporters were all "leftists." He could not even control his own newsmen, he complained, and the front pages of other papers were filled with the evidence of their Democratic bias. To make his case, he brandished a copy of *The New York Times* and pointed out a Page One story as a typical example of "leftist" journalism. The story: a routine monthly account of cost-of-living statistics issued by the Bureau of Labor Statistics, which happened to show a rise on the eve of election.

Time has frequently dismissed the Washington press corps as lopsidedly biased in favor of the Democrats, and a few years back, stated that 85 per cent of its membership was Democratic. This could be true, but it is difficult to prove. Certainly, among reporters covering the Nixon-Kennedy campaign, the large majority personally favored Kennedy. A poll of correspondents in 1952 showed another lopsided majority for Stevenson.

A scholar's questionnaire circulated two years ago produced an inconclusive 273 replies. In them, the reporters classified themselves as follows: Independent, 51 per cent; Democratic, 32 per cent; Republican, 11 per cent; Independent-Democratic, 4 per cent; Independent-Republican, 2 per cent; Socialist, one man.

10

Hail and Farewell

At 10:22 on the morning of January 20, 1961, the two most powerful Republicans in the United States picked their way through the snow to a door in North-west Washington. The blizzard that had paralyzed Washington the night before had passed into the Atlantic, and now as the two men waited quietly for the door to open a sunlight as brilliant and cold as diamond glinted off their high silk toppers. In this strangely arctic morning, with the snow drifted over the azaleas and breaths steam-

226

ing in the Siberian air, one of the most poignant and significant rituals of Washington life was about to begin.

The morning's callers at the home of Vice-President Richard M. Nixon were truly, for this fleeting moment at least, the country's most powerful Republicans, though most Americans would have passed them on the street without recognition. The elder was Styles Bridges, of New Hampshire, dean of Senate Republicans, senior Republican on the Senate Appropriations Committee, chairman of the Senate's Republican Policy Committee, shaper of the Senate's Republican leadership, and spiritual keeper of the Republican party's conservative tradition. He limped slightly because of an arthritic condition in the ankles which had lately been bothering him.

His companion was Representative Charles A. Halleck, of Indiana, Republican leader of the House and as skilled a general as the Republicans had had in a decade. In contrast to Bridges, Halleck's brisk step exuded energy. Behind his big shapeless pugilist's nose, set belligerently between tomato-red cheeks, mischievous blue eyes twinkled in a deceptive suggestion of boyish innocence.

These two were the appointed committee of escort for the Vice-President, whose role in this day's ritual would be the most difficult of all. In a city that enjoys few sports so much as sneering at the fallen, he would have to sit good-naturedly before the masses applauding the accession of the man who had beaten him for the presidency. He must carry it off with no more show of emotion than if he had lost a set at tennis.

Bridges and Halleck remained inside the Nixon home for twenty-three minutes. In the days to come, Bridges would complain about the conduct of Nixon's campaign and about Nixon's campaign isolation from conservative Republicans like himself who had sought futilely to reach him with warnings that he must "slug harder" to win. This, however, was no day for recrimination. At 10:45 Bridges and Halleck emerged with Nixon and his wife, Pat. On election night, television had given the nation an embarrassingly personal portrait of Mrs. Nixon's anguish over the loss, showing her desperate attempts to overmaster her sobs with a good loser's smile while her husband conceded defeat. This was what the television critics called TV's matchless ability to bring the governmental process into the living room in meaningful, educational fashion. Today, however, there was a more advanced lesson for Televisionland, and as the Nixons stepped forth their smiles properly suggested that nothing really terrible had happened.

Mr. Nixon carried his topper. Like the other principals in the day's cast, he seemed ill at ease with this vanishing piece of American haberdashery. The question whether it would be prescribed uniform for the occasion had titillated the Capital for weeks. President Eisenhower had broken the top-hat tradition in 1953 and brought the homburg to glory. In the following eight

228

years the homburg had become a minor symbol of Republicanism, and so the question of headgear was complicated by delicate political considerations, adding further confusion to the muddled symbolism that suffused the hat issue.

On the one hand, the topper was traditionally associated with the caricature of the American plutocrat and, therefore, objectionable to the heirs of Jackson, Roosevelt, and Truman. On the other, it traced a noble lineage back to Lincoln's stovepipe and might, therefore, claim the sanction of something like ceremonial court dress. In recent history, however, it had been prominent in the newsreels of Chamberlain at Munich and of the toppered Japanese diplomats surrendering on the deck of the U.S.S. *Missouri.* Perhaps with this in mind, perhaps mindful that wearing a topper constituted a silent act of obeisance by the homburg Republicans to their Democratic conqueror, Nixon carried his as he left the house. Ironically, it was one he had purchased for his 1953 Inauguration as Vice-President before General Eisenhower decreed homburgs.

At 10:56 A.M. in another part of the Capital the President-elect and his wife, Jacqueline, left their Georgetown house accompanied by Speaker Sam Rayburn and Senator John J. Sparkman, of Alabama, chairman of the Inauguration Committee. Their limousine headed for the White House. Kennedy had not been to bed until nearly four o'clock that morning, having attended a fund-raising gala produced by Frank Sinatra and, afterward, a party given by his father.

The entertainment at the gala had been rich in electronic-age Americana and in instructive example of the republican informality with which the state hails its leaders. In a song composed for the occasion, Miss Helen Traubel, noting the closeness of the election outcome and commenting on the post-election birth of the Kennedys' second child, inquired musically of Mrs. Kennedy why she had not managed the delivery before Election Day. Nat "King" Cole, retelling the story of the campaign in song, had summed up Henry Cabot Lodge's Republican vice-presidential campaign with a verse that began: "Then, Cabot made a boo-boo." After listening to Leonard Bernstein conduct part of Handel's *Messiah*, Kennedy had watched Tony Curtis and Janet Leigh perform a skit that opened with some speculation about whether the United Nations would intervene in the marital troubles of a celebrated Hollywood couple.

The Kennedys arrived at the White House at 11:04 A.M., which was a good bit earlier than customary for the occasion. On the previous evening, President Eisenhower had telephoned Kennedy, noted that the weather promised to be brutal for the noon ceremony next day, and suggested that the Kennedys stop at the White House to warm themselves with coffee before proceeding to the Capitol. They were joined by the Nixons and Mr. and Mrs. Lyndon Johnson.

230

It is difficult to conceive a scene more fittingly symbolic of the enduring and decent continuity of the American system than this unimposing vignette of four men and their wives sipping coffee before exchanging control of the Republic. In Washington, however, it seemed so natural that it scarcely evoked a comment aside from routine news accounts buried deep in chronologies of the day's events. It would have seemed embarrassingly unsophisticated to have marveled that a power so great could be relinquished and assumed without street rioting, firing squads, threats of armed movement, and banishment.

The participants in this recurring ritual had not always been so utterly gracious about it, of course. In 1953, Eisenhower himself had displayed his anger toward Harry Truman by declining to leave his car when he arrived at the White House to escort the retiring President to the Capitol. In other days threats of violence had stalked the occasion. When Lincoln took his oath, secession had already begun. The Cleveland-Blaine election of 1884 had been as close as the Kennedy-Nixon contest of 1960, and some of the more radical Democrats had promised that the government would perish in terror and violence if the Republicans sought to block the Inauguration of the Democrat, Cleveland.

Yet in the end civility had always prevailed, even when grace had failed, and with Lincoln's victory in war, each man down to John Kennedy could claim himself a direct constitutional descendant of George Washington.

For the city these austere reflections were a minor part of the day. As always when a new President is on the threshold, Washington was still reveling in a protracted period of euphoria. As ever in the period of transition, the drab realities were temporarily suspended. Traditionally these few weeks are a season of hope when even the losers are willing temporarily to suspend their greater doubts in service to the national myth that change, after all, is progress, and that progress is blessed. "America hasn't been as happy in three years as they are today," Will Rogers joked when Roosevelt was inaugurated in the desperate spring of 1933. "No money, no banks, no work, no nothing. But they know they got a man there who is wise to Congress. . . . If he burned down the Capitol we would cheer and say, well, at least we got a fire started anyhow."

Washington's excitement over the forthcoming Kennedy administration had been building for two months by the time the Kennedys took coffee with the Eisenhowers at the White House. The campaign, of course, had been a thrilling melodramatic release from the humdrum routine of domestic economics and the depression of international politics, but it was, after all, the country's show rather than Washington's. Its aftermath, the transition of power, was peculiarly Washington's own, offering the kind of sport that only Washingtonians can savor, while renewing the city and changing its air in visible, palpable ways hospitable to Washington's two great delights, gossip and speculation.

Each new President creates his special tone for the city. What would Kennedy's be? Eisenhower, the hero, had represented grandeur and, inevitably, grandeur had been accompanied by withdrawal, aloofness, and, in the men around him, a certain stiffness, a cautious attitude blending reverence and awe. Communicated through the city, the result was stuffiness. The man caught out in an irreverence could scarcely fail to sense the silent indictment of unworthy flippancy returned against him. Piety abounded. Prayer came into its own in a city where Lincoln had complained that because God supplied him no answers he must look to Grant. Golf, long the cartoonist's delight, was taken out of knickers and endowed with respectability.

Kennedy set out to make vigor—invariably pronounced "vigah"—a satisfying substitute for grandeur. Though his golf game was superior to Eisenhower's, the long publicity build-up preceding his nomination and election had emphasized his liking for a rugged bout of touch football with the family. His golf had been so successfully obscured that some of the White House correspondents were surprised to learn that he played at all when he took a post-election holiday in Florida. When news of his game began appearing daily in the press, Pierre Salinger hastened to state that Kennedy would follow a policy of not golfing on White House workdays.

The notion of youthful muscularity in the White House was quick to take hold. Despite Washington's bitterest winter in fifty years, Kennedy insisted upon appearing hatless and without topcoat on the stoop of his Georgetown home to announce each new cabinet appointment. After the Inauguration, when his brother Robert was installed as Attorney General, the city was bemused by reports that the new boss at Justice and his deputy, Byron "Whizzer" White, a former All-American, tossed a football back and forth in the office while threshing out the nation's legal problems.

To Washington's delight, Kennedy brought the presidency out of the White House and into the streets. Under Eisenhower, Washingtonians no more expected to see the President walking past the front door than they did Zeus. But to Kennedy, Washington was a home town, filled with friends and familiar walks. After his second night in the White House he drove to his old house in Georgetown to pick up the Sunday papers, then strolled a few doors up the street and stepped into the house of Benjamin Bradlee, a reporter, yelling: "Anyone at home?"

On Inauguration Night, after attending four Inaugural Balls and seeing most of his exhausted police escort head for home, he astounded Washington by dropping in casually at the home of Joseph Alsop, a columnist, for a pre-dawn bull session. With "vigor" replacing grandeur in the White House it was inevitable that the reverence which the city had assumed under Eisenhower would also pass. Humor, once heretical, enjoyed a revival, sparked by Kennedy's own dry taste for the ironic or pointed phrase. His ubiquity created its own jokes. "Kennedy," went one, "is not only his own Secretary of State and his own Secretary of Defense—he's his own Mrs. Roosevelt." One of Kennedy's own staff men phrased the master comment on the new President's emotional effect on young women: "The Kennedy Administration is going to do for amour what the Eisenhower Administration did for golf."

The change of air that Kennedy would bring had been only remotely evident to Washington during the weeks before the Inauguration. As usual in this period, the city had been absorbed in the overwhelming question of who its new demigods would be; no self-respecting Washington hostess counted her evening complete without a brace of guests who could claim "inside" knowledge of the new President's appointment plans.

For weeks Washington furiously indulged itself in one of its most joyous pastimes, the sport of proving oneself close to the throne by the possession of "inside dope." With the advent of the Kennedy administration it was more fun than it had been in living memory. Unlike most new Presidents, Kennedy and his associates had thousands of social contacts within Washington, so that everybody who could claim to be anybody could cite some plausible source as his guide. Thus, the whole city could play the game.

As in all such things in Washington, the player's object was to acquire status by proving that he had access to the President-elect's circle which provided him with hotter "inside" information than any of his competitive claimants to glory. Style and timing were everything. Style's first requirement demanded that all the principals being speculated about be called by their first names, or better, by their nicknames. This established familiarity. Thus, Governor Abraham Ribicoff, later appointed Secretary of Health, Education, and Welfare, was never "Governor Ribicoff," or just plain "Ribicoff," but always "Abe." In the same way, Kennedy himself was always "Jack." Governor G. Mennen Williams was "Soapy"; Robert A. Lovett, "Bob"; John J. McCloy, "Jack McCloy" (to distinguish him from "Jack"); Chester E. Bowles, "Chet"; and so forth.

In the game competitors also sought to establish their familiarity with the great by manner of delivery. Thus, anyone scored high who said two weeks before the appointment: "Abe is going to get H.E.W.," but he could have raised his status rating even higher by announcing, in a relaxed aside: "I bumped into Bobby today, and it looks like Abe is going to get H.E.W." This established status on two points: (1) Not only did the player know "Bobby," the President's brother, but

(2) "Bobby" apparently thought him worthy of sharing "Jack's" secrets.

For the press, reputations could be made and smashed. *The New York Times*, for example, scored coups by breaking the news that Kennedy would appoint "Bobby" Attorney General and "Luther" Secretary of Commerce. Nevertheless, after *The Washington Post* broke the choicest item of all, Dean Rusk's selection for Secretary of State, Arthur Krock, of *The Times*, commented: "I'd give six Secretaries of Commerce for one Secretary of State."

For those unable to compete at this level, face could be saved with a few tidbits about "Jackie," particularly if they forecast changes in White House décor, and a few words attributable to "Ole Joe," the President-elect's father, were priceless.

Even by the time of the Inauguration it seemed preposterous that the city could ever have been so utterly absorbed in faddist pastime. Such is the transience of Washington moods. At the time the winners and losers were taking coffee at the White House, Kennedy had completed most of his major appointments and the joy had leaked out of the sport for the masses. "What is past is prologue," reads the inscription on the National Archives. "Study the past." Washington, as usual, was bored with the past and studying the future with the happy excitement of a child on the eve of a long journey.

What would it be like? Would the new Congress grant Kennedy a long "honeymoon"? (It didn't even give him a wedding night.) Would the Russians stop being beastly now that there was a new President? (The Russians freed two American fliers who probably should not have been imprisoned to begin with, and then went on, like Russians, being beastly whenever it suited their purpose.) At this moment in the season of hope all questions seemed susceptible of the optimistic "maybe." The arrival of new Presidents is the time for remembering old American truths, that anything is possible, that the surprising happens with incredible regularity.

In the months to come the new Democratic President would recapitulate some of his Republican predecessor's errors in depressing reminder that hope always exceeds grasp, even in the White House. The first meeting of Democratic congressional leaders with the new President was a minor case in point.

After years of hearing the Democrats abuse Hagerty with the charge of trying to "manage the news," the White House correspondents found the Democratic congressmen emerging from the President's office in an abject state of non-communication. Aside from hollow remarks about the usefulness of their palaver, the congressmen, it soon developed, were under orders to say nothing about what had happened within. The reporters pressing for information were referred to Salinger,

Hagerty's Democratic successor, who told them nothing of the slightest news value.

Next day the Republicans had a glorious time on the mimeograph machine and on the Senate floor hooting over what they called Salinger's attempt to "manage the news." Sometimes it seemed that things were more the same than ever. The new Administration was hardly a month old before it found itself caught in one of the notorious and fearful Pentagon "flaps" that had so often afflicted the Eisenhower administration. It originated when the Secretary of Defense, Robert McNamara, insisted in a "background" news conference that there was no "missile gap." By this time there was no precise public idea of what a "missile gap" was, but Kennedy had got much political mileage during his campaign from the Democratic assertion that such a creature existed. McNamara's blithe destruction of the Democratic argument was greeted with glee by the Republicans, and Kennedy, as Eisenhower had often done before him, said that he would have to wait for the findings of a study.

The natural attrition of hope proceeded inevitably at the Capitol, where Kennedy found himself confronted by virtually the same Congress that had found Eisenhower so comfortable and by the same House coalition of Republicans and Southerners which had enforced Eisenhower's deepening conservatism. This dour reality sat heavily on the Kennedy administration from the outset. Enthusiastic pre-election talk of a dynamic hundred days that would give the Administration its momentum died quietly in ˙ December snows. It was replaced by a sober, Ei￉ ￉ower-type explanation of the wisdom of the long ￉ approach.

The utopian civil rights program offered Negroes in the Democratic platform failed to appear in the President's legislative program. Southern support on social and economic bills was too desperately needed. The bulk of the first economic legislation sent to the Capitol consisted of retreaded bills that had been through Congress in 1959–60 and might have been enacted then except for the threat of an Eisenhower veto. Compared with the program of innovation sponsored by Roosevelt in 1933, Kennedy's seemed exceptionally cautious. Republican liberals—those abandoned disciples of the early Eisenhower—found little in the Kennedy program that was objectionable and complained that the President was monopolizing the middle of the road, Eisenhower's old political habitat.

None of these things meant that there would not be important differences of style and accomplishment between the Eisenhower and Kennedy administrations. They were, however, impressive evidences of the accommodation with reality that every President must make in a city that rarely changes its ways and seldom changes its thinking until the country is ready to tolerate it.

Kennedy's chief task as he chatted with Eisenhower in the White House before their ride to the Capitol was to prepare the country to tolerate a change from this charming, comfortable man who had invited him for coffee.

The two men left the White House at 11:30 A.M. The ceremony, as it always is, was moving. True to the Republic's genius for conducting its occasions of pomp on the edge of comic disaster, there was a distracting moment during a long-winded prayer when wiring in the lectern started to burn, sending smoke dancing on the biting wind before the blaze was extinguished. As Eisenhower sat reflecting, topper on his lap, Kennedy began his speech, and the hero-general who had been acclaimed in his lifetime as few men since Caesar, might have heard the heavy page of history quietly turn.

"Let the word go forth from this time and place, to friend and foe alike, that the torch has been passed to a new generation of Americans—born in this century, tempered by war, disciplined by a hard and bitter peace, proud of our ancient heritage . . ."

When it was ended, Eisenhower was driven to a farewell luncheon at the 1925 F Street Club. Nixon, who throughout the ordeal had endured the insolent eyes of his enemies with a smile, was among the guests. Around the corner on Pennsylvania Avenue, hundreds of thousands were gathering with blankets, earmuffs, great-coats, and hip flasks to hail the new chief. Fewer than a hundred loyal bystanders were present to watch the old one and his rejected heir make their departure.

When the luncheon ended, Eisenhower and Nixon emerged together from the club. Nixon nodded toward the small group of watchers as they began to applaud. "We've still got a few left," he said. Eisenhower grinned and entered his limousine and a thin patter of applause marked his adieu to Washington.

A sentimentalist, listening later to the thundering ovation given the new President upon his arrival at the White House, might have reflected that Washington, for all her pretensions to rank as a great lady among world capitals, still has the instinctive reflexes of a harlot. Her eye, to be sure, is perpetually set on the main chance, her favors reserved for today's hero, her heart either closed to the fallen or exultant in his discomfort. When fortune rides with the mighty, he can have no quality so loathsome that it cannot be made a virtue. When last year's hero fails, Washington packs him off to obscurity in the cruel ice of her indifference and throws herself at his conqueror.

And yet, for all her cruelty, she acquires her new masters and discards the old peaceably and according to good legal form, and she rarely fails to cry at the funeral of either. There is a good deal to be said for that.

A NOTE ABOUT THE AUTHOR

RUSSELL WAYNE BAKER was born in 1925 in Loudoun County, Virginia. After getting his B.A. in English from Johns Hopkins University in 1947, he started work as a police reporter for the Baltimore *Sun* that summer, and two years later went on to general assignments and rewrite. In 1952 he went abroad as the *Sun*'s London correspondent, then back to Washington for the *Sun* in 1954, switching at the end of that year to *The New York Times*'s Washington Bureau. Mr. Baker has covered the White House, the State Department, Congress, both parties' political conventions of 1956 and 1960, including Eisenhower's presidential campaign of 1956 and both the Kennedy and Nixon campaigns of 1960; also Eisenhower's heart attack in Denver, the Senate civil rights filibuster of 1960, sundry inaugurations and investigations. Mr. Baker's present assignment for the *Times* is the Senate. He lives in Washington with his wife, the former Miriam Emily Nash, and their three children.

October 1961

A   NOTE   ON   THE   TYPE

THE TEXT OF THIS BOOK was set on the Linotype in JANSON, a recutting made direct from the type cast from matrices long thought to have been made by Anton Janson, a Dutchman who was a practicing type-founder in Leipzig during the years 1668-1687. However, it has been conclusively demonstrated that these types are actually the work of Nicholas Kis (1650-1702), a Hungarian who learned his trade most probably from the master Dutch type-founder Dirk Voskens. The type is an excellent example of the influential and sturdy Dutch types that prevailed in England prior to the development by William Caslon of his own incomparable designs, which he evolved from these Dutch faces.

This book was composed, printed, and bound
by H. WOLFF, New York. The paper was manufactured
by P. H. GLATFELTER, Spring Grove, Pa.
Typography and binding design
by GUY FLEMING.